Rib ticklers
& choux-ins

GLYNN
PURNELL

Rib ticklers
& choux-ins

**110 SENSATIONAL RECIPES
FROM STEAKS+BAKES TO CHEESECAKES**

PHOTOGRAPHY BY PETER CASSIDY

KYLE BOOKS

For Fezza, AKA Kerry, as always, the unsung hero, my childhood sweetheart. And the 'P' unit, Oliver, Esmè, Vincent and Whoops, my babies.

In memory of my beautiful friend Nic, taken from us too soon. Loved and never forgotten. Wife to Pete and mother of my godson Harvey. xxxx

First published in Great Britain in 2016 by
Kyle Books, an imprint of Kyle Cathie Ltd
192–198 Vauxhall Bridge Road
London SW1V 1DX
general.enquiries@kylebooks.com
www.kylebooks.co.uk

10 9 8 7 6 5 4 3 2 1

ISBN 978 0 85783 339 6

EDITOR JUDITH HANNAM
EDITORIAL ASSISANT HANNAH COUGHLIN
COPY EDITOR JO RICHARDSON
DESIGNER HELEN BRATBY
PHOTOGRAPHER PETER CASSIDY
FOOD STYLIST ROSIE REYNOLDS
PROP STYLIST IRIS BROMET
PRODUCTION NIC JONES AND GEMMA JOHN

A Cataloguing in Publication record for this
title is available from the British Library.

Colour reproduction by f1 colour
Printed and bound in China by C&C
Offset Printing Co., Ltd.

6 INTRODUCTION

8 IS IT BREAKFAST, LUNCH OR BRUNCH?

34 TAKE-AWAY, TAKE TIME, NIBBLES, SNACKS + BITES

54 1,2,3,4,5, ONCE I CAUGHT A FISH ALIVE!

82 THIS LITTLE PIGGY WENT TO MARKET

112 A MOMENT ON THE LIPS

150 TO HAVE + TO HOLD, BUT DON'T GET TOO KNEADY

168 BITS + STUFF + CHEEKY TRICKS

INDEX

FUN, FUN, FUN!

That is what cooking should be. Yes you should strive for perfection, and yes cooking should be taken seriously, but it is also about making people happy. It is a gift. There are not many things that make you feel as special as food does (apart from sex, of course, but that's another book!).

Running the Bistro is so different from a Michelin Star Restaurant. The idea is the same, but the delivery is poles apart. It's about meeting, chatting, sharing. It's about the buzz of the bar, the sound of cocktails being shaken, the hustle and bustle.

There are so many rules in restaurants, the do's and don'ts. The Bistro is more relaxed, but has some all its own:
1. Try something new, we won't disappoint.
2. Gents, always offer your seat to a lady.
3. Perfection takes time, please be patient.
4. No crying or yawning, we are neither your mother nor your bed.
5. If you don't like your drink let us know & we'll make one that you do.
6. Drunkenness is prohibited, please don't act like an amateur.
7. If you are drunk, call it a night, we will call you a cab & we suggest you don't call your ex.

Like the recipes in this book, they're designed to ensure people have a good time. There is some sharing food, some fine food, some rustic food but most of all fun food!

ENJOY!

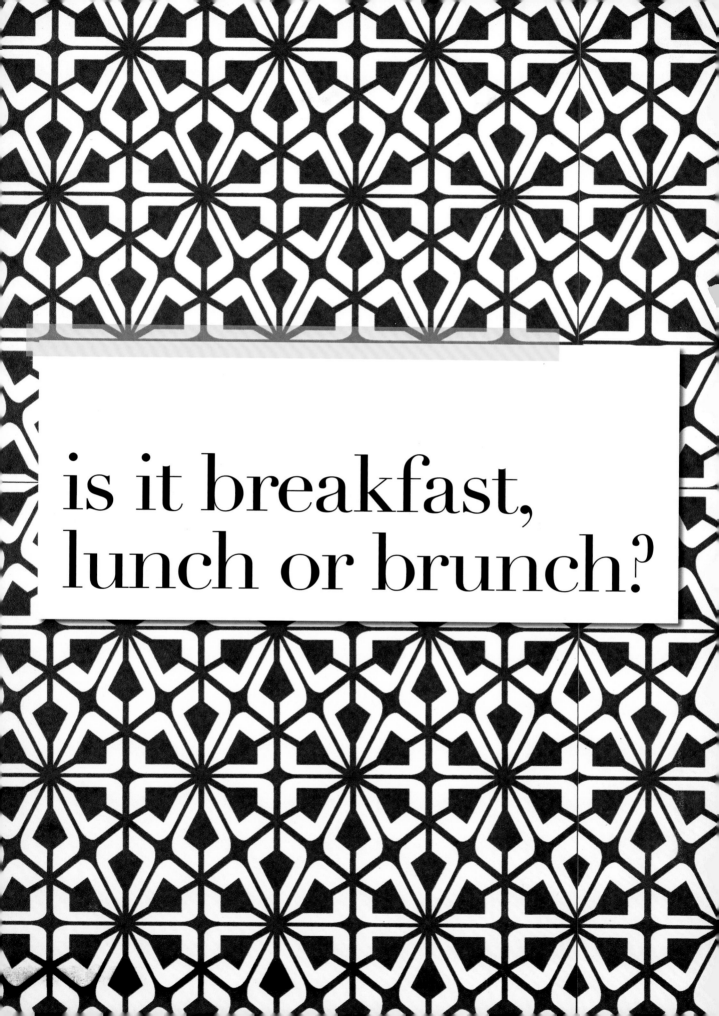

is it breakfast,
lunch or brunch?

I love breakfast, but when does it stop? Never, I say! It becomes brunch, and then lunch, and then really, really late breakfast since there is no word for eating between lunch and dinner. Anyway, I love breakfast, and I think it should be served all day, whatever you call it. My fondest memories are of breakfast as a child, waking up on a Sunday (though not all the time!) to the smell of bacon and the sound of my dad cooking up a storm, and then all of us tucking into a feast fit for a king.

SWEET FRUIT SALAD

Fruit is a great way to start the day. Choosing exotic fruits, both acidic and sweet, makes this a great brunch dish too, particularly when teamed with the creamy coconut sorbet. If the fruit is ripe it is a dream come true. It also makes a great pud.

FOR THE POACHED PINEAPPLE

3 LITRES PINEAPPLE JUICE, PLUS EXTRA
   IF NEEDED
3 STAR ANISE
3 BAY LEAVES
2 VANILLA PODS, SPLIT LENGTHWAYS AND
   SEEDS SCRAPED OUT
200G LIGHT SOFT BROWN SUGAR
3 LARGE PINEAPPLES
3 CINNAMON STICKS

In a large saucepan, bring the pineapple juice, star anise, bay leaves, vanilla seeds and sugar to a simmer.

Meanwhile, remove the skin and eyes from the pineapples. Halve each pineapple across the equator and remove the core with an apple corer. Snap the cinnamon sticks in half and insert half a stick into each pineapple half in place of the core.

When the poaching liquid has reached simmering point, carefully place the pineapples in the liquid, adding more pineapple juice to cover if needed. Place a cartouche (circle of greaseproof paper) over the pineapples and poach for 45 minutes–1 hour, or until a paring knife can penetrate the pineapple with a little resistance. Be careful not to boil.

When ready, remove the pan from the heat and leave the pineapples to cool in the liquid.

Once cool, store the pineapples in an airtight container in the fridge until needed. They will keep for up to three weeks. For maximum flavour, poach the pineapples two days before using.

FOR THE COCONUT SORBET

800G COCONUT PUREE
200G COCONUT MILK
4 TEASPOONS MALIBU (OR ANY
   COCONUT-BASED WHITE RUM)
JUICE OF 1 LEMON
110G STOCK SYRUP (SEE PAGE 143)

Whisk all the ingredients together in a large mixing bowl.

Cover and leave the mixture to mature in the fridge for a minimum of 12 hours and up to 24 hours.

Churn in an ice-cream maker according to the manufacturer's instructions until frozen. Store in the freezer in a lidded freezer-proof container for up to 6 months.

FOR THE LYCHEE PUREE

425G CAN LYCHEES IN LIGHT SYRUP,
    DRAINED AND SYRUP RESERVED
1 VANILLA POD, SPLIT LENGTHWAYS
½ XANTHAN GUM

Roughly chop the lychees and put in a saucepan with one-quarter of the reserved syrup from the can. Add the split vanilla pod and bring to the boil, then simmer for 5 minutes.

Whizz in a blender until smooth, then add the xanthan gum and whizz until the required texture is achieved. If the mixture is too stiff to blend, add more of the reserved syrup.

Pass the purée through a fine sieve, cover and refrigerate until required.

FOR THE MANGO PUREE

1 MEDIUM MANGO, PEELED, FLESH DICED
JUICE OF ½ LIME
SALT AND POWDERED GINGER, TO SEASON

Place the mango and lime juice in a saucepan with 100ml water. Season with salt and powdered ginger and cook down until soft, about 20 minutes.

Pass the purée through a fine sieve, cover and refrigerate until required. It can also be frozen and stored for 3 months.

FOR THE FRUIT

3 KIWI FRUIT, PEELED
1 LARGE MANGO, STONED AND PEELED
1 DRAGON FRUIT, PEELED

Slice and dice the fruit and mix together in a bowl.

TO SERVE

2 PASSION FRUIT, CUT IN HALF, SEEDS
    AND JUICE SCOOPED OUT
ZEST OF ½ LIME

Slice the poached pineapple thinly, then arrange in a ribbon along the left-hand side of the plate.

Arrange the fruit mixture to the right of the pineapple

Place a scoop of coconut sorbet on top of the diced fruit.

Add a dot of mango purée above and a dot of lychee purée below.

Drizzle passion fruit seeds and juice over the pineapple and finish with the lime zest.

MUESLI, SEEDS + FRUIT MIX

We all love a full English, a sausage or an omelette, a fried egg or a nice buttery croissant or pain au chocolat, but for everyday it's probably wiser to go for something healthier. The options can be a bit boring, so I've tried to fancy them up a bit. If you don't want to make as much, halve the quantities.

MAKES 50
PRE-MIXED
PORTIONS

FOR THE MUESLI

- 1.4KG JUMBO PORRIDGE OATS
- 400G SUNFLOWER SEEDS
- 400G PUMPKIN SEEDS
- 200G SESAME SEEDS
- 200G BLUE POPPY SEEDS
- 300G DEMERARA SUGAR
- 400G WHEAT GERM
- 400G RUNNY HONEY
- 300G OLIVE POMACE OIL
- 160G READY-TO-EAT DRIED APRICOTS, DICED
- 160G DRIED APPLE RINGS, DICED
- 160G DRIED PINEAPPLE, DICED
- 100G DRIED STRAWBERRIES
- 100G DRIED RASPBERRIES
- 400G RAISINS
- 300G FLAKED ALMONDS, TOASTED
- 300G ALL-BRAN

Preheat the oven to 150°C/gas mark 2.

Wearing disposable gloves, mix together the porridge oats, seeds, sugar and wheat germ thoroughly in a large mixing bowl.

Mix the honey and pomace oil together and add to the bowl, then mix again thoroughly with your hands, ensuring that all the dry ingredients are evenly coated.

Divide the mixture between two large roasting tins and toast in the oven for 15–20 minutes, stirring every 5 minutes, until aromatic and golden. Be careful to avoid over browning the mixture, as this will result in a harsh, bitter taste. Remove from oven and leave to cool.

Once completely cooled, place all the toasted mixture in a large bowl and add the remaining ingredients, mixing thoroughly with your hands.

Divide the muesli between four large vacuum food sealer bags and seal with a vacuum sealer to remove the air, but not excessively, as this will crush the muesli. Store in a dry place for up to three months.

FOR THE SEED MIX

- 600G PUMPKIN SEEDS
- 400G SUNFLOWER SEEDS
- 200G BLUE POPPY SEEDS
- 200G SESAME SEEDS

Mix all the ingredients thoroughly in a large mixing bowl.

Store in an airtight container in a dry place.

FOR THE DRIED FRUIT MIX

- 500G READY-TO-EAT DRIED APRICOTS, DICED
- 500G DRIED APPLE RINGS, DICED
- 500G DRIED PITTED DATES, DICED
- 500G SULTANAS
- 500G GOLDEN RAISINS

Mix all the ingredients thoroughly in a large mixing bowl.

Store in an airtight container in a dry place.

JUICES

Wash, prepare and then process the ingredients for each juice through a juicer according to the manufacturer's instructions. Mix together well and serve immediately, or store in an airtight container in the fridge for up to 12 hours.

GREEN JUICE

½ HEAD OF CELERY, TRIMMED
1 LEMON, PEEL AND PITH REMOVED
1 PINEAPPLE, SKIN, EYES AND CORE REMOVED
50–75G SPINACH
1 FENNEL BULB, TRIMMED
15G FRESH GINGER, PEELED
½ PUNNET (ABOUT 250G) WHITE GRAPES (OPTIONAL,
    IF A SWEETER FLAVOUR IS REQUIRED)
50G GREEN KALE
3 PEARS

GREEN FENNEL JUICE

3 FENNEL BULBS, TRIMMED
½ HEAD OF CELERY, TRIMMED
3 PEARS, PEELED AND CORED
2 LEMONS, PEEL AND PITH REMOVED
1 CUCUMBER
50–75G SPINACH
1 PINEAPPLE, SKIN, EYES AND CORE REMOVED
½ PUNNET (ABOUT 250G) WHITE GRAPES

RED JUICE

2 LARGE BEETROOT, PEELED
½ HEAD OF CELERY, TRIMMED
2 CARROTS, TOPS REMOVED
3 PEARS, PEELED AND CORED
15G FRESH GINGER, PEELED
1 PUNNET (ABOUT 200G) BLUEBERRIES
    (OR DOUBLE UP THE QUANTITY IF
    BLACKBERRIES AREN'T AVAILABLE)
1 PUNNET (ABOUT 150G) BLACKBERRIES
1 ORANGE, PEEL AND PITH REMOVED
1 PUNNET (ABOUT 500G) RED GRAPES

OEUFS COCOTTE

A cocotte is the dish that the egg is cooked in, so oeuf cocette is, yes you got it, an egg cooked in a cocotte – no flies on you! The classic flavours to add are ham and cheese, which work really well. Sometimes it's best not to mess. This classic method – or to some people a new method – of cooking, produces a tasty breakfast, lunch or starter.

40G BUTTER
4 EGGS
160G MANCHEGO CHEESE, DICED
4 SLICES OF SMOKED HAM
4 FLAT-LEAF PARSLEY LEAVES

SERVES **4**

Preheat the oven to 180°C/gas mark 4.

In the oven, warm 10g butter in each of four 15cm pots or small ovenproof frying pans.

Crack an egg into the foaming butter, then add 40g Manchego, one slice of ham, torn into pieces, and one parsley leaf, torn into pieces.

Place the pans in the oven for 2–3 minutes.

Serve in the pan on a plate, with warm buttered muffins or toast.

HEN'S EGGS ARE GREAT BUT TO TAKE THIS DISH TO THE NEXT LEVEL USE DUCK EGGS – FAB!

EGG YOLK + SALMON TARTLETS

The combination of smoked salmon, light, salty cheese and an aromatic chive background is dynamite. And, yes! They will explode – with egg yolk – so mind your chin!

MAKES 6

1 SHEET OF READY-ROLLED PUFF PASTRY, DEFROSTED IF FROZEN
150G SMOKED SALMON, CHOPPED
2 TABLESPOONS CHOPPED SPRING ONIONS
2 TABLESPOONS CHOPPED CHIVES
6 EGG YOLKS, BEATEN
1 TABLESPOON DOUBLE CREAM
30G PARMESAN CHEESE, GRATED

Preheat the oven to 150°C/gas mark 2.

Roll out the pastry to a thickness of 2–3mm. Using an 8cm round pastry cutter, cut out six circles and use to line a six-hole muffin tin. Place a second six-hole muffin tin on top and weight down with baking beans.

Bake for 10–15 minutes, or until golden brown.

Turn the pastry cases out of the tin and leave to cool on a wire rack. Increase the oven temperature to 180°C/gas mark 4.

When the pastry cases are cool, divide the smoked salmon, spring onions and chives between them. Mix the egg yolks and cream together, then pour over to cover. Sprinkle with the grated Parmesan and return to the oven for 2 minutes.

Serve warm, but beware – they will explode!

POTATO OMELETTE WITH SMOKED SALMON

A Spanish omelette, really. Or a frittata, which, by the way, is an Italian word that means 'to fry' or something like that, so you can add anything to it – meat, cheese, vegetables, peppers – you get the idea. It's a lovely dish any time of the day. We often have it at home as a brunch or early tea, which means dinner where I am from. If brunch is between breakfast and lunch, what is between lunch and dinner? Linner?

SERVES 4

FOR THE OMELETTE
500G MASHED POTATO, WARM
2 TABLESPOONS PLAIN FLOUR
3 EGGS, PLUS 3 EGG WHITES, WHISKED
  TO STIFF PEAKS
100ML DOUBLE CREAM
SALT AND FRESHLY GROUND
  BLACK PEPPER
4 TABLESPOONS VEGETABLE OIL

FOR THE GARNISH
100G SMOKED SALMON
4 TABLESPOONS SOURED CREAM (OR
  CREME FRAICHE OR MASCARPONE)
50G ROCKET LEAVES
50G MIZUNA LEAVES
1 SMALL LEMON, QUARTERED
20 CAPERS

Preheat the oven to 190°C/gas mark 5.

Place the warm mashed potato in a large mixing bowl. Add the flour, whole eggs and cream, and mix together well.

Fold the whisked egg whites into the mixture, and season with salt and black pepper.

On the hob, heat 1 tablespoon vegetable oil in each of four 15cm blini or small ovenproof frying pans until smoking. Pour one-quarter of the potato mixture into each pan and cook until beginning to colour.

Place the pans in the oven for 4–5 minutes, then flip each omelette onto a plate.

Garnish each omelette with one-quarter of the smoked salmon, 1 tablespoon soured cream, a grinding of black pepper, one-quarter of the rocket and mizuna leaves and a lemon wedge, then sprinkle over five capers.

SPICED RED PEPPER +TOMATO SOUP

Red, bright, spicy and alive, this is what this soup is. Sweet with a silky texture, it can also be served cold if you want. I also use it as a pasta base, but primarily, for me, it's a delicious brunch snack or a terrific starter, and so easy to do.

SERVES 6–8
(MAKES
3 LITRES)

SPLASH OF VEGETABLE OIL
3 ONIONS, SLICED
1 GARLIC BULB, CLOVES SEPARATED,
   PEELED AND CHOPPED
2 RED CHILLIES, CHOPPED (WITH SEEDS)
50G BUTTER
1 TABLESPOON SMOKED PAPRIKA
6 RED PEPPERS, DESEEDED AND CHOPPED
2 TABLESPOONS PLAIN FLOUR
100ML WHITE WINE VINEGAR
2 TABLESPOONS CASTER SUGAR
800ML BOILING WATER
1.3KG CANNED TOMATOES, WHIZZED IN
   A BLENDER TO A PUREE
15G SALT

Heat the oil in a large saucepan and sweat the onions over a medium–low heat for about 10 minutes until soft but not coloured.

Add the garlic and chillies, and sweat for a few minutes.

Stir in the butter with the smoked paprika and cook for 2 minutes.

Add the red peppers and cook for about 10 minutes until soft. Add the flour and cook, stirring, for 2 minutes.

Stir in the vinegar, sugar and water, and simmer for 10 minutes.

Add the blended tomatoes and cook for a further 10 minutes.

Add the salt, then whizz in a blender until smooth and pass through a sieve before serving either hot or cold.

DOUBLE CREAM SCRAMBLED EGGS WITH SMOKED SALMON, SALMON EGGS + WATERCRESS

Fab for breakfast at any time of year, but particularly at Christmas, when I have them with shampoo – not for your hair but to drink! (Champagne to the rest of you.)

SERVES 2

50G BUTTER

4 EGGS, BEATEN

50ML DOUBLE CREAM

2–4 SLICES OF BREAD, TOASTED

4 SLICES OF SMOKED SALMON

15G SALMON EGGS

SALT AND FRESHLY GROUND BLACK PEPPER

WATERCRESS, TO GARNISH

Melt the butter in a saucepan over a gentle heat. Add the eggs and cook, stirring them constantly, until they start to thicken. Remove the pan from the heat and bring the eggs together with a whisk.

Fold in the cream and immediately spoon the scrambled eggs onto the toasted bread. Lay over the smoked salmon and spoon over the salmon eggs.

Season with salt and a turn from the pepper mill, garnish with watercress and serve immediately.

TARTARE OF ASPARAGUS + FENNEL CLOUD

Tartare means raw, well sort of, and also (without the 'e') a mineral build-up on your teeth. You'll be pleased to know that this one is raw asparagus and is a play on the more usual steak tartare. Also, it's not an actual cloud, but it feels like one and looks like one so, with romance in mind, let's call it one. Life is too short not to.

FOR THE FENNEL CLOUD
50G GRANULATED SUGAR
1 GELATINE LEAF, SOAKED IN COLD WATER
    FOR 5 MINUTES
320ML FENNEL JUICE, FROM 3 LARGE
    FENNEL BULBS, MIXED WITH 5G ASCORBIC
    ACID, 50G CASTER SUGAR AND 5G SALT
18G POWDERED EGG WHITE
    (I USE ALBÚMINA)
2 TEASPOONS PERNOD
5G FENNEL POLLEN (OPTIONAL)

FOR THE ASPARAGUS AND FENNEL TARTARE
3 WHITE ASPARAGUS SPEARS, TRIMMED,
    PEELED AND SLICED
3 GREEN ASPARAGUS SPEARS, TRIMMED,
    PEELED AND SLICED
SALT AND GROUND GINGER
1 TABLESPOON OLIVE OIL
1 LEMON
½ FENNEL BULB, TRIMMED
1 TABLESPOON CHOPPED TARRAGON

FOR THE GREEN ASPARAGUS
60G BUTTER
3 GREEN ASPARAGUS SPEARS, TRIMMED
2 TABLESPOONS REDUCED BEEF STOCK

WATERCRESS, TO GARNISH

For the fennel cloud, heat 100ml water and the sugar gently in a saucepan until the sugar has dissolved.

Remove the pan from the heat, add the squeezed-out gelatine leaf and leave until melted, stirring occasionally.

In the bowl of a stand mixer fitted with the whisk attachment, whisk the fennel juice mixture and Albúmina together by hand to combine the ingredients. Switch on the mixer and begin whisking on a low speed, then gradually increase the speed.

When the mixture has nearly tripled in volume, decrease the speed and add the gelatine mixture. Whisk on high a speed until stiff peaks form.

Pour in the Pernod and whisk through, then pour the cloud mixture into a freezer-proof dish lined with cling film, spread it flat and sprinkle with the fennel pollen (if using). Place in the freezer for 6 hours, or until frozen, and store in the freezer until required.

For the tartare, mix the white and green asparagus together, and season with the salt and ground ginger. Add the olive oil and a squeeze of lemon juice, grate in the fennel and mix the ingredients together. Add the tarragon and set aside.

For the green asparagus, heat a frying pan, then add the butter and asparagus, fry over a medium–high heat for about 2 minutes until the asparagus is nearly cooked, then squeeze in a little lemon juice and add the beef stock. Cook for a further 2 minutes.

Place the sautéed asparagus onto one side of the plate and the tartare on the other side, then spoon the fennel cloud on top of the tartare and garnish with watercress. Serve immediately.

SERVES 4

CHEESE + POTATO PIE 'GRATIN'

My mom used to make this gratin for me, and I loved it, so I thought I would do one for you. My mom would often finish the dish by scattering the top with a packet of plain crisps or sliced tomato, depending on the time and her mood, I suppose. You can change the cheese if you want to, but this is a true Ma Purnell classic.

SERVES 4–6

200G CLEAN, LARGE-GRAINED INDUSTRIAL
   WHITE ROCK SALT
6 MEDIUM–LARGE BAKING POTATOES,
   SKIN ON, WASHED
SPLASH OF VEGETABLE OIL
1 MEDIUM ONION, CHOPPED
KNOB OF BUTTER, PLUS 60G
310G HARD MATURE CHEDDAR
   CHEESE, GRATED
100ML DOUBLE CREAM
100ML MILK
1 TABLESPOON CHOPPED PARSLEY
1 TABLESPOON CHOPPED SPRING ONIONS

Preheat the oven to 180°C/gas mark 4.

Sprinkle the salt onto a baking tray and place the potatoes on top.

Bake the potatoes for 1½ hours, or until they are soft.

Remove the potatoes from the oven and leave to cool slightly, then cut in half, scoop out the potato into a bowl and beat until smooth. Reserve the skins.

Heat the oil in a flameproof casserole dish, add the onion and cook over a medium heat for 2–3 minutes. Add the knob of butter and cook for a further 2 minutes, then remove from the heat.

Add the potato, 250g of the cheese, the remaining 60g butter, the cream, milk, parsley and spring onions, then mix together and spread out in the casserole dish, smoothing the surface.

Cut the potato skins into strips and scatter over the potato mixture, then cover with the remaining 60g cheese.

Bake for 20 minutes, or until golden brown. Serve with a salad or as a side dish for meat or fish.

MIX THE CHEESE UP TO GIVE IT A CHANGE. TRY USING A BIT OF BLUE!

BALEARIC PRAWNS WITH CHILLI BUTTER

I love these, and so do most people when they get the chance to eat them – it's a mega favourite at the Bistro. I also cook them at home in a massive terracotta dish that Val, a family friend, gave me when we visited her in Tenerife. I love my holidays with my missus and the little people, and regard this as my holiday dish cooked in my holiday pot. Enjoy!

SERVES 4

500G CLARIFIED BUTTER
2 RED CHILLIES, SLICED
2 GREEN CHILLIES, SLICED
3 GARLIC CLOVES, SLICED
800G RAW PEELED MEDIUM PRAWNS
10G BASIL, CHOPPED
10G PARSLEY, CHOPPED
1 LEMON, CUT INTO WEDGES

Heat the clarified butter in a saucepan with the red and green chillies and garlic over a high heat until they float to the top.

Add the prawns, put the lid on the pan and cook for 2 minutes.

Finish with the herbs and a squeeze of lemon.

TOM YUM SOUP

Tom yum is a deliciously flavoursome soup, a little different from the usual, plus it can be kept in the freezer or made and gorged down when cooked. Often, I serve it with raw tuna or some big, plump prawns, or even beef tartare as a main course. It is so fresh and light, as wonderful chilled in summer as it is warm in winter with extra chillies. It's a foreign dish but, as we say here in Brum, it's bostin!

SPLASH OF SUNFLOWER OIL
4 TABLESPOONS THAI TOM YUM PASTE
    (I USE MAI SIAM)
8 TOMATOES
1 SHALLOT, FINELY SLICED
4 LEMONGRASS STALKS, SPLIT AND
    ROUGHLY CHOPPED
4 CORIANDER ROOTS OR STEMS FROM
    2 BUNCHES OF CORIANDER
100G FRESH GALANGAL, PEELED AND SLICED
8 LIME LEAVES
JUICE OF 2 LIMES
100G TAMARIND PASTE
2 RED CHILLIES, SLICED
75G THAI PALM SUGAR
200G UNCOOKED GLASS NOODLES
2 TABLESPOONS FINELY CHOPPED
    CORIANDER
75ML THAI FISH SAUCE
2 CARROTS, PEELED AND SLICED
    INTO THIN STRIPS
ABOUT 350G BEANSPROUTS,
    CUT IN HALF
ABOUT 200G MANGETOUT,
    FINELY SLICED
25G TOASTED BLACK AND
    WHITE SESAME SEEDS
8 SLICES OF PICKLED GINGER

Heat the oil in a large saucepan and gently sweat the tom yum paste for 1 minute.

Pour in 1.5 litres cold water and gently bring to the boil.

Score a cross in the base of each tomato and remove the eye.

Blanch the tomatoes in a saucepan of boiling water for 10 seconds, then drain and refresh in iced water.

Remove the skins of the tomatoes and add the skins to a large saucepan. Cut the tomatoes into quarters and scrape the seeds into the pan with the skins. Cut the tomato flesh into chunks and set aside.

Add the shallot, lemongrass, coriander roots or stems, galangal, 6 of the lime leaves, the lime juice, tamarind paste, 1 red chilli and the palm sugar to the tomato skins and seeds in the pan.

Pour the boiling tom yum stock into the pan and gently simmer for 10 minutes.

Pass through a sieve into a clean saucepan and keep warm.

Cook the noodles in boiling water according to the instructions on the packet. Drain and refresh in iced water, then cut them in half.
Bring the stock back up to a gentle simmer.

Add the diced tomato, remaining 2 lime leaves and red chilli, the coriander and fish sauce to the saucepan, then pour in the hot stock and keep hot.

Mix together the remaining vegetables, noodles, sesame seeds and pickled ginger in a large bowl, then divide between four serving bowls.

Pour over the tom yum soup and leave for 2 minutes before serving.

SERVES 4

DUCK RILLETTES

Otherwise known as confit de carnard. Reminds me of my trip to Bordeaux, when we drove in a little French car to stay at my friend's grandmother's house in the Pyrenees. She had no electricity, but she had her own ducks. So we ate her foie gras by candlelight, as well as roasted green beans with garlic and crispy confit duck, all served in the pans they were cooked in. We drank great wine and clear eau de vie, which she had made with prunes, and it blew our heads off. We drank and laughed, and by the end of it I could speak French – or at least I thought I could.

MAKES
10 X 125ML
JARS

5 DUCK LEGS
125G DUCK FAT, MELTED
150G DRAINED GHERKINS, FINELY CHOPPED
75G DRAINED CAPERS, FINELY CHOPPED
1½ TABLESPOONS CHOPPED PARSLEY
75ML BRANDY
ZEST AND JUICE OF 1 ORANGE
1 TEASPOON QUATRE EPICES
SALT AND FRESHLY GROUND BLACK PEPPER
250G SALTED CLARIFIED BUTTER
10G GREEN PEPPERCORNS, DRAINED
   AND CHOPPED

Preheat oven to 220°C/gas mark 7.

Submerge the duck legs in the melted duck fat in a deep roasting tin and place in the oven for 2 hours, or until the meat is tender.

Remove the legs from the fat, reserving the fat, and leave until cool enough to handle.

Pick the duck meat from the bones, taking care to remove all remaining bones, skin and gristle from the meat. Place the meat in a large mixing bowl and add 250ml of the reserved duck fat, the gherkins, capers, parsley, brandy and orange zest and juice. Season with the quatre épices, salt and black pepper, and mix well, then taste and adjust the seasoning if necessary.

Divide the mixture between ten 125ml sterilised preserving jars and chill in the fridge for 2 hours, or until set.

Mix the clarified butter and green peppercorns together, then spoon a thin layer on top of the mixture in each jar and return to the fridge until required. The rillettes will keep in the fridge for 3–5 days.

Remove from the fridge around 30 minutes before eating and serve with salad and some toasted Granary Bread (see page 160).

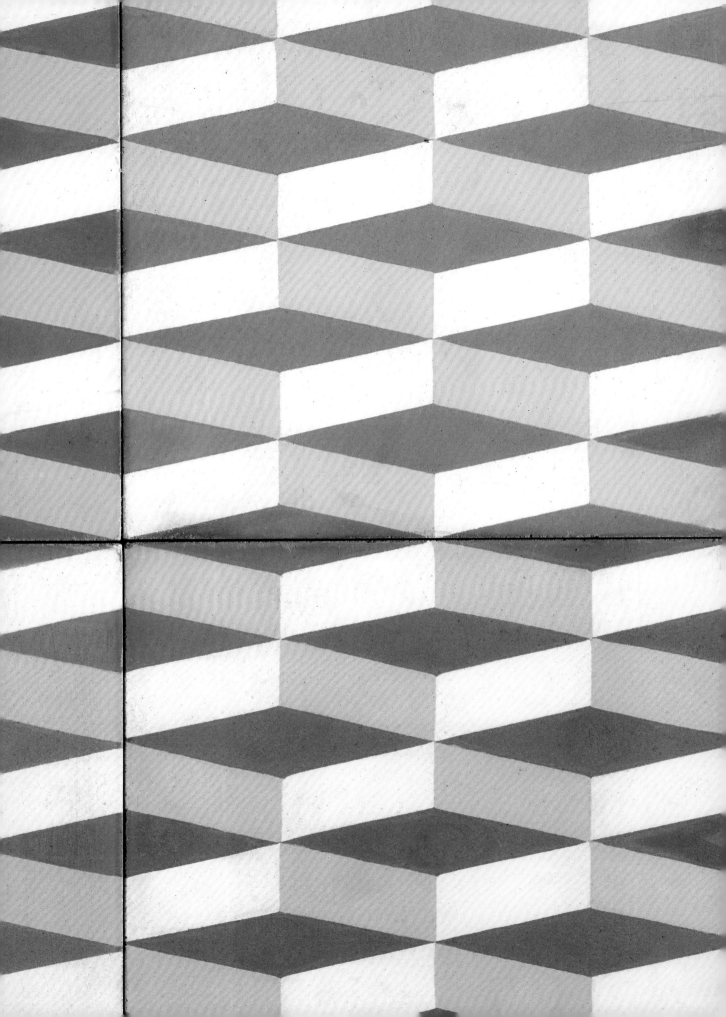

take-away, take time, nibbles, snacks & bites

As a young chef, I would run around, not really thinking, rushing, sweating and just good old-fashioned panicking. One lunchtime, a salesman came in. The gentleman's name was Lionel, and he was selling toilet rolls and cleaning stuff. At first, he just stood watching me, shaking his head. After a while, he called me over.

'Slow down,' he said.

'I'm busy!' I said.

'Take your time and think about it,' Lionel replied.

'I can't,' I said, 'I'm in the shit!'

'Let me tell you a story,' he replied. 'Once upon a time there were two bulls in a field – an old bull and a young bull. The young bull said to the old bull, "Let's run down the field and shag one of those cows." The old bull replied, "Let's walk down there and shag them all."' The moral of the story is, take your time, don't go charging in. Lionel is no longer with us, but I will always remember his advice. RIP my friend, never forgotten.

CHILLI LEMON + ROSEMARY SAVOURY POPCORN

As amazing as popcorn is, here I've made it truly amazing. Well, really good! A savoury popcorn with salt, chilli, lemon and a sprinkle of rosemary. Have as a little nibble with pre-dinner drinks, as a cheeky canapé or just in a massive bowl in front of the TV.

3 TABLESPOONS VEGETABLE OIL
200G POPCORN KERNELS
150G CASTER SUGAR
15G SALTED BUTTER
1 TEASPOON CHILLI POWDER
1 TEASPOON CHOPPED ROSEMARY LEAVES
ZEST OF 1 LEMON

Heat the oil in a large, lidded saucepan over a medium heat. Once the oil is hot, add a couple of popcorn kernels and wait for them to pop – this will indicate that the oil is ready.

Add all the kernels to the pan, put the lid on and keep shaking that pan, dudes!

Once all the kernels have popped, turn them out onto a tray.

Heat the sugar in a separate large, heavy-based saucepan over a medium heat until it starts to melt, then stir gently with a heatproof spatula to evenly caramelise the sugar until a light caramel forms and the sugar crystals have all dissolved.

Add the butter with the chilli powder, and once melted, toss in the popcorn until evenly coated with the caramel.

Toss in the rosemary and lemon zest and serve.
BANG 'POP' WALLOP!

GRILLED SZECHUAN-STYLE CHICKEN SKEWERS

Think of kebabs, and you probably think of getting pissed with your mates, rolling around on the floor and then finishing off the evening with a big fat doner kebab (early 90s for me. I've grown up since – well, sort of). These kebabs, or skewers as we now call them, are great as a cheeky indulgence on a drunken night in, either as a starter or a snack. It's a lot safer to roll around in the comfort of your own home!

SERVES 6

1 TABLESPOON MIRIN
1 TABLESPOON CASTER SUGAR
75ML LIGHT SOY SAUCE
150G SZECHUAN BEAN SAUCE
1 TABLESPOON FISH SAUCE
1 LARGE RED CHILLI, DICED
1 TABLESPOON GRATED FRESH GINGER
2 GARLIC CLOVES, CRUSHED
8 CHICKEN THIGHS, SKINNED, BONED AND
   CUT INTO 2.5CM DICE
8 LARGE SPRING ONIONS
2 TABLESPOONS (PURE) SESAME OIL
2 TEASPOONS TOASTED SESAME SEEDS

TO SERVE
STEAMED JASMINE RICE OR COOKED
   EGG NOODLES
LEMON WEDGES

Mix together the mirin, sugar, soy, bean and fish sauces, chilli, ginger and garlic in a saucepan. Gently warm through over a low heat until the sugar has dissolved.

Remove the pan from the heat and leave to cool.

Add the chicken to the marinade and leave to marinate, covered, in the fridge for 2 hours.

Drain the chicken, then cut the spring onions into pieces of a similar size to the chicken.

Thread a piece of chicken onto a wooden or metal skewer (if using wooden skewers, presoak in water for about 30 minutes), followed by a piece of spring onion. Continue, alternating the ingredients, until you have threaded six skewers.

Cook the skewers on a hot barbecue or griddle pan, or under a grill for about 8 minutes, turning frequently, until the chicken is cooked through.

Brush the skewers with the sesame oil, sprinkle over the toasted sesame seeds and serve with steamed jasmine rice or cooked egg noodles and lemon wedges for squeezing over.

NOW, THE QUESTION IS, ARE YOU A BREAST OR A THIGH MAN? IF YOU'RE TALKING CHICKEN, IT HAS BE THIGHS. THEY'RE THE BEST PART OF THE CHICKEN AND SO TASTY. THE SKIN AND THE FAT ARE FAB.

CRISPY SCALLOP + PRAWN BALLS WITH STICKY AROMATIC SAUCE

Together, the words scallops, prawns and crispy sound WOW. Then throw in a ball – BANG! A fab crispy treat, with a little bit of spice and a little dippy sauce to go with them.

VEGETABLE OIL, FOR DEEP-FRYING
750G RAW PEELED PRAWNS
1 TABLESPOON DASHI STOCK
2 EGG WHITES, LIGHTLY BEATEN
⅔ TABLESPOON CORNFLOUR
SALT
150G SHELLED AND CLEANED SCALLOPS
 (SEE PAGE 80)
1 RED CHILLI, SLICED
2 TEASPOONS CHOPPED CORIANDER
1 TEASPOON DARK SOY SAUCE
1 TABLESPOON SAKE
1 TABLESPOON MIRIN
1 TABLESPOON FISH SAUCE
1 TEASPOON GROUND GINGER, PLUS
 EXTRA TO SEASON

FOR THE STICKY AROMATIC SAUCE
175G CASTER SUGAR
200ML DARK SOY SAUCE
1 TABLESPOON SHAOXING RICE WINE
50ML MIRIN
50ML MALT VINEGAR
50G PALM SUGAR
50ML FISH SAUCE
1 GARLIC CLOVE
½ LEMONGRASS STALK
30G PEELED FRESH GINGER
2 RED CHILLIES, SPLIT LENGTHWAYS

For the sauce, mix together all the ingredients in a saucepan and simmer for 5–10 minutes until the mixture coats the back of a spoon.

Remove the pan from the heat and leave to cool.

Heat the oil for deep-frying in a deep-fat fryer or deep saucepan until the temperature reaches 180°C (use a food thermometer).

Put the prawns, dashi stock, egg whites, cornflour and a pinch of salt in a blender and whizz together until well blended. Add the remaining ingredients and blend again until well combined.

Turn the mixture out of the blender into a bowl and roll into 4cm balls with your hands.

Deep-fry the balls, in batches, for about 2 minutes until golden brown. Remove and drain well on kitchen paper, then season with salt and ground ginger.

Serve the scallop and prawn balls warm alongside the sauce. They can also be served with rice as a main course.

SERVES 4 OR 2 GREEDY PEOPLE

CHICKEN GOUJONS [PROPER NUGGETS!] WITH SMOKED PAPRIKA MAYO

Nuggets get such bad press because most burger and fast-food places don't do them justice. Here is a great recipe to prove nuggets – sorry goujons – can be tasty.

SERVES 2–4

VEGETABLE OIL, FOR DEEP-FRYING, PLUS 200ML FOR THE MAYO
2 LARGE BONELESS, SKINLESS CHICKEN BREASTS
150G PLAIN FLOUR
4 EGGS
150G FINE SOFT WHITE BREADCRUMBS
1 TEASPOON SMOKED PAPRIKA
SALT AND FRESHLY GROUND BLACK PEPPER

Heat the oil for deep-frying in a deep-fat fryer or deep saucepan until the temperature reaches 180°C (use a food thermometer).

Cut the chicken breasts lengthways into strips about 3cm wide.

Put the flour in a shallow bowl, two of the eggs, beaten, in a second bowl and the breadcrumbs in a third bowl.

Roll the chicken in the flour, then dip in the beaten egg and coat in the breadcrumbs. Repeat the coating process a second time until the chicken is completely coated. (This method also works well with fish – fish fingers!)

For the mayo, separate the remaining two eggs. Whisk the smoked paprika into the egg yolks. Add the oil very gradually in a slow, steady stream, whisking constantly, until the mixture thickens – if the oil is added too quickly, the mixture will split. Season with salt and black pepper.

Deep-fry the chicken strips for about 5 minutes until cooked through and golden. Remove from the oil and drain on kitchen paper, then season with salt and black pepper. Serve immediately with the mayo as a great snack or a cheeky little starter.

SALT+PEPPER CHICKEN WINGS

Finger lickin' chicken! Oh, maybe I can't say that? Too bad. Already have! This is my wife's favourite starter. You can use drumsticks or ribs instead, but for me wings are the best. Cheap and delicious, so easy to make and well worth the fuss. You can add more chilli for an extra kick or add a splash of lime or soy to mix it up.

20 CHICKEN WINGS
2 TEASPOONS SALT
2 TEASPOONS CRUSHED BLACK
  PEPPERCORNS
2 TEASPOONS CRUSHED WHITE
  PEPPERCORNS
VEGETABLE OIL, FOR DEEP-FRYING,
  PLUS 2 TABLESPOONS
3 TABLESPOONS CORNFLOUR
1 TABLESPOON CUSTARD POWDER
1 TEASPOON CHILLI POWDER
1 MEDIUM ONION, SLICED
1 RED CHILLI, SLICED
1 GREEN CHILLI, SLICED
4 SPRING ONIONS, CHOPPED
2 TEASPOONS CHOPPED CORIANDER
SQUEEZE OF LEMON JUICE

Put the wings in a saucepan, cover with 2 litres cold water (or enough to cover the wings) and simmer for 10 minutes.

Drain the wings in a colander and leave to cool, then season with the salt and crushed black and white peppercorns.

Heat the oil for deep-frying in a deep-fat fryer or deep saucepan until the temperature reaches 180°C (use a food thermometer).

Mix together the cornflour, custard powder and chilli powder in a shallow bowl.

Roll the wings in the cornflour mixture and then deep-fry for 5 minutes until golden brown. Remove from the oil and drain on kitchen paper.

Heat the remaining 2 tablespoons oil in a large frying pan over a medium heat, add the onion and chillies and cook for 3 minutes until soft. Add the wings and stir to coat with the onion and chillies.

Toss in the spring onions and coriander, and finish with a squeeze of lemon juice. Serve as a great take-away-style snack.

SERVES 4

THIS IS A WING DISH, BUT YOU COULD USE SOME JUICY THIGHS INSTEAD OR A DRUMSTICK.

DUCK SPRING ROLLS

In this recipe I am using duck, but you can change it up if you like with prawns, beef, chicken, pork or leftover roast. Ideal for a Monday tea or a Sunday snack, or as part of a snack/nibble fest!

MAKES 10

2 TABLESPOONS COCONUT OIL
100G CARROT, SHREDDED
100G SAVOY CABBAGE, SHREDDED
50G SPRING ONIONS, SHREDDED
4 TABLESPOONS HOISIN SAUCE
25G SESAME SEEDS
3 TABLESPOONS CHINESE FIVE-SPICE POWDER
2 TEASPOONS CHOPPED CORIANDER
100G BEANSPROUTS
¼ TEASPOON CHILLI POWDER
150G CONFIT DUCK LEG, SHREDDED (YOU CAN ALSO USE COOKED CHICKEN LEG MEAT OR BEEF)
10 SHEETS OF SPRING ROLL PASTRY
1 EGG WHITE
1 TEASPOON CORNFLOUR
VEGETABLE OIL, FOR DEEP-FRYING

Heat the coconut oil in a saucepan and sweat the carrot, cabbage and spring onions over a gentle heat until slightly broken down.

Stir in the hoisin sauce, sesame seeds, five-spice powder, coriander, beansprouts, chilli powder and duck.

Lay out one sheet of pastry on the work surface. Mix the egg white and cornflour with a little cold water to create a paste. Brush the pastry sheet with the paste.

Pack the duck mixture into a strip along the edge of the pastry sheet nearest to you, leaving a narrow margin of pastry at the sides.

Fold in both sides of the pastry, covering the ends of the mixture, then roll the pastry away from you, keeping the mixture tightly wrapped. Repeat with the remaining pastry sheets and filling.

Heat the oil for deep frying in a deep-fat fryer or deep saucepan until the temperature reaches 180°C (use a food termometer). Deep-fry the rolls, in batches, until golden. Remove from the oil and drain on kitchen paper. Uncooked rolls can be frozen for future use.

CHILLI PEANUT NOODLES

Hot chillies, crunchy nuts. Sounds like a Carry On film! Anyway, this is a really tasty starter or snack, or serve with meat or seafood, such as jumbo fried prawns.

SERVES 2

150G DRIED EGG NOODLES
2 TABLESPOONS SESAME OIL
1 TABLESPOON GROUNDNUT OIL
1 TABLESPOON CHOPPED RED CHILLI
2 TABLESPOONS CHOPPED PEANUTS
1 TABLESPOON LIGHT SOY SAUCE
SEA SALT AND GROUND GINGER
1 TABLESPOON CHOPPED CHIVES

Cook the noodles in a saucepan of boiling water for 2 minutes, then drain in a colander.

Heat the sesame and groundnut oils in a large frying pan, add the chilli and peanuts and toast gently for 2 minutes.

Add the drained noodles to the pan and stir in the soy sauce.

Season with salt and ground ginger and sprinkle in the chives. Serve immediately.

EGG NOODLES WITH POTTED SHRIMPS

Sometimes in life things can seem too hard or not worth the effort, but these are well and truly not, and are. They taste great and are so easy to make and you'll look like the bollocks when you serve them to your friends.

SERVES 4

300G PLAIN FLOUR, PLUS EXTRA
    FOR DUSTING
3 EGGS, BEATEN
SPLASH OF OLIVE OR SESAME OIL
SALT
200G POTTED SHRIMPS
1 TEASPOON FISH SAUCE
1 TEASPOON DARK SOY SAUCE
FRESHLY GROUND BLACK PEPPER
1 TABLESPOON CHOPPED CHIVES

Put the flour in a bowl and add the beaten eggs and oil, then mix well with your hands until the mixture comes together, or pulse the ingredients in a food processor until they come together.

Tip the dough out onto a board and knead into a smooth ball. Alternatively, use a stand mixer fitted with a dough hook if you prefer.

Wrap the dough in clingfilm and leave to rest in the fridge for a minimum of 1 hour.

Flatten the dough with your hands and dust lightly with flour on both sides, then run the dough through a pasta machine on its widest setting five times, folding it in half after each rolling, until smooth.

Run the dough through the pasta machine again at the widest setting, then work through the narrowing settings in turn, lightly dusting with flour when necessary to prevent it sticking, until you have a thin sheet.

Meanwhile, bring a large saucepan of salted water to the boil.

Fit the pasta machine with a noodle-cutting attachment and slice the pasta sheet into noodles.

Add the noodles to the pan of boiling water and cook for 2–3 minutes, then drain in a colander.

Put the noodles in a large bowl and add the potted shrimps (including the butter) and the fish and soy sauces.

Toss to combine and season with salt and black pepper, then finish with the chives. Serve the noodles on their own or with Spiced Pork Belly (see page 92).

SALT-BAKED POTATOES WITH CHORIZO MAYONNAISE

Baking veg in salt is not new, though mine are great – my potatoes that is. I love the smell when they are cooking and the meaty mayo really makes this snack/starter (or side dish) a real centrepiece for a party. Even better is giving someone the chance to give them a good smack to get them out.

675G CLEAN, LARGE-GRAINED INDUSTRIAL
    WHITE ROCK SALT
4 EGG WHITES, BEATEN
4 MEDIUM–LARGE WAXY POTATOES,
    SKIN ON, WASHED

FOR THE MAYONNAISE
400G CHORIZO, DICED
300ML VEGETABLE OR RAPESEED OIL
3 MEDIUM EGG YOLKS
2 TABLESPOONS WHITE WINE VINEGAR

FOR THE ESCABECHE
1 MEDIUM BEETROOT, PEELED
1 GOLDEN BEETROOT, PEELED
1 MEDIUM CANDY BEETROOT, PEELED
1 MEDIUM TURNIP, PEELED
1 SMALL (BUT NOT BABY) FENNEL BULB,
    TRIMMED
100ML CHARDONNAY VINEGAR
300ML VEGETABLE OR RAPESEED OIL
3 SPRIGS OF THYME
1 GARLIC CLOVE, CRUSHED
BUNCH OF WATERCRESS
FRESHLY GROUND BLACK PEPPER

Preheat the oven to 180°C/gas mark 4.

Mix together the rock salt and egg whites, then cover the base of an ovenproof dish with some of the salt mixture and place the potatoes on top. Completely cover with the remaining salt.

Bake the potatoes for 40 minutes.

Meanwhile, for the mayonnaise, fry the chorizo in a deep saucepan over a low heat until lightly coloured, then add the oil and cook slowly for 5–10 minutes.

Remove the pan from the heat and leave to cool for 10 minutes, then pass the contents through a fine sieve to separate the chorizo and oil, reserving both.

Whisk together the egg yolks and white wine vinegar in a bowl. Add the chorizo oil very gradually in a slow, steady stream, whisking constantly, until the mixture thickens. Set aside.

For the escabeche, using a mandoline if you have one, thinly slice the beetroot, turnip and fennel, then put in iced water.

Mix together the Chardonnay vinegar and oil in a medium bowl to make a vinaigrette, then add the sprigs of thyme and garlic.

Drain the vegetables and mix with the vinaigrette.

Place a spoonful of mayonnaise on each plate. Dress with the vegetables and garnish with watercress. Sprinkle with the chorizo and season with black pepper.

Turn out the salt-baked potatoes and smash the salt casing to release the potatoes. Serve alongside the mayonnaise and vegetables.

SERVES 4

SALT-BAKED POTATOES WITH
CHORIZO MAYONAISSE
+ESCABESH OF VEGETABLES

SWEET SPICY STICKY RIBS

Ribs are brilliant. I love them, my kids love them, my staff love them. I don't know anyone that doesn't love them; If you do, feed them – force-feed them – and you'll change their mind. Trust me, or block me on Facebook and Twitter!

SERVES 7

2 TABLESPOONS VEGETABLE OIL
1 ONION, THINLY SLICED
2 GARLIC CLOVES, THINLY SLICED
4 CLOVES
½ CINNAMON STICK
1 TEASPOON BLACK ONION SEEDS
1 TEASPOON GROUND GINGER
1 RACK OF PORK BELLY RIBS,
   CUT INTO INDIVIDUAL RIBS
150G CASTER SUGAR
50ML WHITE WINE VINEGAR
50ML DARK SOY SAUCE
1 LARGE TABLESPOON TOMATO KETCHUP
2 MEDIUM–HOT CHILLIES, ROUGHLY CHOPPED
1 TABLESPOON CHOPPED CORIANDER
SQUEEZE OF LIME JUICE

Heat the oil in a large saucepan over a medium heat. Add the onion and garlic and cook until softened but only lightly coloured.

Add the cloves, cinnamon, onion seeds and ginger to the pan and then add the ribs. Cover all the ingredients with 2 litres cold water (or enough to cover the ribs), then simmer for 30–40 minutes until the meat is tender.

Drain the ribs (you can reserve the cooking liquid to make a sauce for another dish).

Heat a large frying pan, add the sugar, vinegar and soy sauce and boil the mixture until reduced to a thick consistency.

Add the ketchup to the pan, then stir in the ribs, coating well with the glaze. Add the chillies, coriander and a squeeze of lime juice, then serve. The ribs can be served with egg noodles or jasmine rice.

A LITTLE TIP – INSTEAD OF RIBS BUY PORK BELLY ON THE BONE. THAT WAY YOU GET FREE RIBS AND PROBABLY THE BEST PART OF THE PIG.

1, 2, 3, 4, 5, once I caught a fish alive!

People seem to be scared of fish. That's okay for sharks, I guess, but you're not likely to find many of those at home, or at the Bistro. Unless, of course, you're playing cards with my mother-in-law! Scared of cooking fish is what I mean. Here, though, are plenty of simple fish dishes for you to try, plus a few more complicated ones, for when you've got the hang of it.

And, just for the record, NO! Fish don't have fingers! How many times?

BAKED COD WITH A SECRET GREEN CRUST
[NOT SO SECRET ANYMORE!]

This idea isn't new but, as I've said before, I love a classic. Adding smoked salmon and horseradish to the crust gives a depth of flavour and a little edge. So, spread the word. Or keep it a secret!

70G FLAT-LEAF PARSLEY
100G SLICES OF WHITE BREAD,
  CRUSTS REMOVED
50G SMOKED SALMON
70G SALTED BUTTER
JUICE OF ½ LEMON
20G CREAMED HORSERADISH
1 TABLESPOON VEGETABLE OIL
4 X 150G PORTIONS OF SKINLESS
  COD FILLETS

Preheat the oven to 180°C/gas mark 4.

Pulse together the parsley and bread in a food processor to form fine crumbs, then add the smoked salmon, butter, lemon juice and horseradish and whizz to make a paste.

Spread the paste out onto a sheet of greaseproof paper to a thickness of 1cm. Cover with another sheet of greaseproof paper and place in the freezer for 4–6 hours minutes until firm.

Rub a baking tray with the oil and place the fillets, evenly spaced, on the tray.

Take the paste out of the freezer and cut it into pieces the same shape as the fish. Place the 'crust' on top of each fillet. The remaining crust can be returned to the freezer to be used another day.

Bake the fish for 12–15 minutes until it is cooked through and the crust is bright green. Serve with steamed greens.

BAKED COD WITH A
SECRET GREEN CRUST

BAKED HAKE + CLAMS IN GREEN SAUCE

Hake is an amazing, meaty fish, and British too. For some reason, though, we've fallen out of love with it and the Spanish buy most of ours now. This dish – from the Basque region – is designed to entice you into trying hake. The rich buttery green sauce is delicious and brings back fond memories of my time in this part of Spain.

SERVES 4

2 CELERY STICKS, THINLY SLICED
½ FENNEL BULB, TRIMMED AND THINLY SLICED
½ ONION, THINLY SLICED
2 BAY LEAVES
SPRIG OF THYME
4 X 125G HAKE FILLETS, SKIN ON
1.2KG LIVE CLAMS, WASHED
150ML WHITE WINE
100ML DOUBLE CREAM

FOR THE PARSLEY BUTTER
½ BUNCH OF PARSLEY
1 GARLIC CLOVE, CHOPPED
150G SALTED BUTTER, SOFTENED

TO GARNISH
PARSLEY LEAVES
WATERCRESS LEAVES

For the parsley butter, put all the ingredients in a blender and whizz together until well blended, then transfer to a container, cover and chill in the refrigerator for 6 hours or overnight.

Preheat the oven 180°C/gas mark 4.

Cut a piece of foil 60 x 40cm and line it with a 30cm square of greaseproof paper so that the fish doesn't stick to the foil.

Mix together the celery, fennel, onion, bay leaves and thyme, then sprinkle evenly over the paper.

Place the hake fillets on top. Bring up the two long sides of the foil and fold over at the top, then fold over the two sides to form a half-moon-shaped parcel, crimping to seal.

Place the parcel on a baking tray and bake for 10–12 minutes.

Heat a saucepan on the hob, add the clams, then the wine and put the lid on. Gently shake the pan and leave for 30 seconds, or until all the shells have opened (discard any that remain closed). Remove the clams from the pan and set aside, leaving the cooking liquid in the pan.

Simmer the cooking liquid for 2 minutes or until reduced by half.

Whisk the chilled parsley butter into the reduced cooking liquid and add any liquid from the baked fish, then finish with the cream.

Place fish on a serving dish and pour over the green sauce and clams. Garnish with parsley and watercress leaves.

ROAST MONKFISH TAILS WITH BUTTERED LETTUCE, +FROZEN APPLE

Monkfish is one of the most fantastic things, both to eat and cook. It's meaty and very versatile; I almost treat it like meat. Roasting it on the bone gives it a natural feel. Serving it with cider, turnips and buttered lettuce really lifts it, but the showstopper (which will make you look like a right smart-arse) is grating the frozen – yep, frozen – apple over the top of the dish at the table.

1 TABLESPOON VEGETABLE OIL
2 MEDIUM MONKFISH TAILS, BONE IN, SKINNED
1 BAY LEAF
4 SPRIGS OF THYME
2 GARLIC CLOVES, PEELED
100ML HOT FISH OR VEGETABLE STOCK
350ML DRY CIDER
3 MEDIUM TURNIPS, PEELED AND SLICED INTO DISCS
4 SAGE LEAVES
1 ICEBERG LETTUCE, CUT IN HALF AND LEAVES SEPARATED
20 MINT LEAVES
SQUEEZE OF LEMON JUICE
200G SALTED BUTTER
FRESHLY GROUND BLACK PEPPER
1 GREEN APPLE, FROZEN FOR 24 HOURS

SERVES 4

Preheat the oven to 180°C/gas mark 4.

Heat the oil in a large flameproof casserole dish. Add the monkfish and cook until coloured on both sides. Add the bay leaf, thyme, garlic and stock.

Place the dish in the oven for 15 minutes, or until the monkfish is cooked through.

While the monkfish is cooking, bring the cider to a simmer in a saucepan. Add the turnip and sage leaves and cook for 2–4 minutes minutes until the turnips are tender but not too soft.

Put the lettuce and mint leaves in a bowl.

Remove the casserole dish from the oven and lift the monkfish out onto a plate. Add a squeeze of lemon juice and leave to rest.

Add the butter to the casserole dish to deglaze, scraping up all the sediment with a wooden spoon, but don't cook the butter. Pour the warm buttery juices over the lettuce and mint. Cover the bowl with clingfilm and give it a shake.

Using a sharp knife, cut against the bone all the way down either side of each monkfish tail to give two long fillets.

To serve, divide the turnips evenly between four plates and season with black pepper. Place a monkfish fillet on each plate on top of the turnip discs. Spoon the turnip cooking juices over the fish. Transfer the lettuce and mint to a serving bowl. Just before serving, grate the frozen apple over the monkfish and turnips – do this at the table as a showpiece!

SCALLOPS WITH LIME, WASABI CRUMBLE +WATERCRESS

Everyone loves cooked scallops, but they're just as tasty raw. It's important, though, that they are mega fresh, straight out of the shell, and given a quick wash. The lime adds freshness, and the wasabi a little heat, Japanese style.

SERVES 4

FOR THE WASABI CRUMBLE
300ML SUNFLOWER OIL
200G HORSERADISH ROOT, PEELED
   AND GRATED
90G TAPIOCA MALTODEXTRIN
50G WASABI PEAS

FOR THE CUCUMBER KETCHUP
1 CUCUMBER, PEELED AND
   ROUGHLY CHOPPED
30ML CIDER VINEGAR
30G GRANULATED SUGAR
5G AGAR AGAR
½ TEASPOON WASABI PASTE

FOR THE SCALLOPS
4 SHELLED AND CLEANED LARGE SCALLOPS
   (SEE PAGE 80)
ZEST AND JUICE OF 2 LIMES
SALT AND GROUND GINGER

WATERCRESS, TO GARNISH

For the wasabi crumble, put the oil in a saucepan, add the horseradish and leave to infuse over a low heat for 2 hours, ensuring that the temperature of the oil doesn't rise above 100°C (use a food thermometer).

Remove the pan from the heat and leave to cool. Once cold, pass through a fine sieve.

Pour 100ml of the horseradish oil into a jug blender, add 45g of the tapioca maltodextrin and whizz together. With the blender running, gradually add the remaining 45g tapioca maltodextrin until a light crumble forms. Tip the crumble out into a bowl.

Pulse the wasabi peas in the blender and then stir through the crumble.

For the cucumber ketchup, whizz the cucumber in the blender for 5 minutes, or until smooth. Pass through a sieve into a bowl and then return to the blender.

Heat the vinegar and sugar in a saucepan, stirring until the sugar has dissolved, then add to the cucumber. Bring 100ml water to the boil in a saucepan, then whisk in the agar agar and cook over a medium heat, stirring, for 2 minutes.

Start to blend the cucumber mixture and then, with the blender running, add the agar agar solution. Once it is fully incorporated, pass through a fine sieve into a bowl, cover and leave to set in the fridge for 2 hours.

Return the set cucumber mixture to the blender with the wasabi paste and blend until smooth. Set aside.

Slice the scallops very thinly into rounds and add to a bowl with the lime zest and juice. Season to taste with salt and ground ginger. Leave to stand for 10 minutes.

To serve, lay the scallops out on the plate, spoon over the crumble and finish with a few sprigs of watercress. Serve the ketchup on the side for people to help themselves.

ROAST SALMON WITH SALSA VERDE, NOODLES +GREMOLATA

Salmon can be a little bit boring – it always seems to be paired with a cream sauce or mash – so here is a classic summer dish that can be served either as a main course or a nice little starter. Smash it on the BBQ or bake the fish if you want, whatever suits the mood you're in! You can add or take away your least favourite herb from the salsa (which works well with grilled meat too, or as a dip) or spice it up with extra chilli. Plus you'll look like you know what you're doing when you plonk it down and say, 'SALSA VERDE!'.

SERVES 4

400G DRIED VERMICELLI RICE NOODLES
4 SALMON FILLETS, SKIN ON, PIN BONES
    AND SCALES REMOVED
SALT AND FRESHLY GROUND BLACK PEPPER
DRIZZLE OF OLIVE OIL

FOR THE SALSA VERDE
½ CUCUMBER, PEELED AND DICED
1 TEASPOON CHOPPED PARSLEY
1 TEASPOON CHOPPED CORIANDER
1 TEASPOON CHOPPED MINT
1 TEASPOON COARSE-GRAIN MUSTARD
ZEST AND JUICE OF 2 LEMONS,
    MIXED TOGETHER
2 TEASPOONS CAPERS
2 TEASPOONS DICED GHERKINS
2 TEASPOONS PINE NUTS, TOASTED
250ML OLIVE OIL, PLUS EXTRA TO GARNISH
DICED AVOCADO, TO TASTE (OPTIONAL)

FOR THE GREMOLATA
3 SLICES OF WHITE BREAD,
    CRUSTS REMOVED
ZEST OF 1 LEMON
10G PICKED PARSLEY LEAVES

For the salsa verde, mix together the cucumber, herbs, mustard, lemon zest and juice, capers, gherkins and pine nuts in a bowl and add the olive oil to bind. Add the avocado (if using) and season to taste with salt and black pepper.

For the gremolata, pulse the ingredients in a food processor to form fine crumbs. Set aside.

Put the noodles in a deep tray and cover with boiling water. Leave to soften for 3–5 minutes, then drain and refresh in cold water. Refrigerate until required.

Heat a frying pan over a medium heat, add the salmon, skin-side down, and cook for 3 minutes. Turn over and cook for a further 2 minutes.

While the salmon is cooking, plunge the noodles into a saucepan of boiling salted water for 1–1½ minutes, then drain. Put in a bowl, then add the salsa verde, toss together and season to taste with salt and black pepper.

To serve, divide the noodles between four bowls. Place the salmon fillets on top and sprinkle the fish with the gremolata. Garnish with a drizzle of olive oil and a turn of the pepper mill.

IF YOU LEAVE THE SKIN ON WHEN YOU ROAST YOUR SALMON IT GIVES IT A FABULOUS CRISPINESS AND THE BUTTERY FLESH IS STUNNING.

MALAYSIAN FISH CURRY

I have never been to Malaysia, but I imagine it's a wonderful place. The reason why I am cooking this is because a Malaysian guy used to fix my car. It was a right bucket! Anyhow, one day he called me in for lunch and it was amazing. A little rustic, but wow! This is my take on what he served. The car, by the way, has gone now.

SERVES 4

2 GARLIC CLOVES
3 SHALLOTS
ABOUT 4CM PIECE OF FRESH GALANGAL, PEELED
2 TABLESPOONS FISH PASTE
1 TABLESPOON FISH SAUCE
SPLASH OF VEGETABLE OIL
2 RED CHILLIES
2 GREEN CHILLIES
12 CURRY LEAVES
1 TEASPOON SWEET PAPRIKA
1 TEASPOON GROUND TURMERIC
1 TEASPOON GROUND GINGER
1 TEASPOON CHILLI POWDER
300ML COCONUT MILK
2 TABLESPOONS TAMARIND PASTE
130ML HOT FISH STOCK (SEE PAGE 185)
2 LEMONGRASS STALKS
1 TABLESPOON CASTER SUGAR
1KG SKINLESS COD FILLETS, DICED

Put the garlic, shallots and galangal in a blender and whizz together, then add the fish paste, fish sauce and about 4 tablespoons cold water and whizz again to make a paste.

Heat the oil in a saucepan and stir in the red and green chillies, curry leaves, paprika, turmeric, ginger and chilli powder. Add the garlic, shallot and galangal paste and cook over a medium heat for 3 minutes until dry.

Stir in the coconut milk, tamarind paste and fish stock, then drop in the lemongrass. Simmer for 8–10 minutes.

Add the sugar and cod and simmer for 5 minutes until cooked through. Serve with bread, naan or roti canai.

SMOKED HADDOCK WITH CREME FRAICHE MASH

Anyone that knows me knows that I love smoked haddock. It gives me a warm glow inside. Memories both of the markets as a boy and my Mom's cooking. Enjoy!

4 X 130G PORTIONS OF SMOKED
  HADDOCK FILLETS
20G MILD CURRY POWDER
VEGETABLE OIL, FOR RUBBING
300G MASHED POTATO
50G CREME FRAICHE
JUICE OF 1 LIME
SALT AND FRESHLY GROUND BLACK PEPPER
4 EGG YOLKS
50G CHIVES, CHOPPED
20ML CURRY OIL
CORIANDER SHOOTS, TO GARNISH

Preheat the oven to 180°C/gas mark 4.

Dust the haddock with the curry powder and rub with vegetable oil.

Heat a large ovenproof frying pan over a medium heat, and when hot, add the fish and cook on one side for 3–5 minutes.

Place the pan in the oven for 2 minutes, or until the fish is cooked through.

Meanwhile, heat up the mash in a saucepan and whisk in the crème fraîche and lime juice until a loose, rich, acidic mash is achieved, then season with salt and black pepper.

Heat a large, wide saucepan of water to 80°C, add the egg yolks, one at a time, and poach, in batches, for 2 minutes, then immediately remove with a slotted spoon and drain on kitchen paper.

Serve the mash onto each plate, sprinkle with the chives and garnish with a little of the curry oil.

Place the fish on the plates and top each with a poached egg yolk. Garnish with coriander shoots and the remaining curry oil before serving.

SERVES 4

SCORCHED BABY SQUID PROVENCAL

I love squid. Love the texture of it, the smell as it cooks, how strange it looks, but how amazing it is. And squid with ham is a beautiful combo. The Provençal bit comes from the red peppers and olives, which remind me of sunshine, holidays and the odd glass to wash everything down ... God, I need a holiday!

SERVES 3

3 MEDIUM SQUID TUBES, CLEANED
9 SLICES OF SERRANO HAM
3 ROASTED RED PEPPER HALVES
9 SUN-DRIED TOMATOES, CUT IN HALF
50G OLIVE TAPENADE MIXED WITH
  2 TABLESPOONS OLIVE OIL
10G PUNNET MICRO BASIL
10G PUNNET MICRO ROCKET

Preheat the grill to medium.

Slice the squid into rings and cook under the grill for 1½ minutes.

Divide the squid rings between three plates and arrange three slices of Serrano ham on each plate.

Garnish each serving with a roasted red pepper half and six sun-dried tomato halves.

Spoon small amounts of the olive tapenade mixture into the gaps.

Finish with the micro basil and rocket.

I LOVE COOKING AND EATING PRETTY MUCH ALL TYPES OF SQUID, WHATEVER THEIR SIZE, BUT THE BABY ONES ARE THE SWEETEST.

MUSSELS IN CIDER WITH PARSLEY + TRUMPET MUSHROOMS

I've both worked in, and travelled around, a few places in Europe and everywhere I go it's classic mussels marinière – marinara if you're Italian – usually served with bread, beer and chips. WOW, love them, and the beer (goes without saying). I have dropped cider in mine, along with keeping to the traditional flavours of garlic, etc. It's nice to give a classic dish a twist, but don't mess about too much. Wise words my friend, wise words.

SPLASH OF VEGETABLE OIL
3 SHALLOTS, SLICED
1 GARLIC CLOVE, SLICED
2KG LIVE MUSSELS, SCRUBBED
   AND DEBEARDED
4 TABLESPOONS CHOPPED PARSLEY,
   STALKS RESERVED
300ML GOOD-QUALITY DRY CIDER
   (PLUS A GLASS TO DRINK!)
50G BUTTER
300G TRUMPET MUSHROOMS, CLEANED
   AND CUT IN HALF
FRESHLY GROUND BLACK PEPPER

SERVES 4

Heat the oil in a large saucepan, add the shallots and sweat over a gentle heat until softened, then add the garlic.

Add the mussels and parsley stalks, then pour over the cider.

Put the lid on and cook over a medium heat, shaking the pan occasionally, for 3–4 minutes, or until all the shells have opened (discard any that remain closed). Drain the mussels and reserve the cooking liquid.

Melt the butter in a separate large pan, add the mushrooms and fry for a minute or so.

Add the mussel cooking liquid and cook for 1 minute until reduced, then add the mussels, some in their shells and some out. Throw in the chopped parsley and season with a few turns of the pepper mill. Serve in a large bowl with some skinny fries.

SEA BASS WITH PISTOU, ARTICHOKES +SUN-DRIED TOMATOES

The fillet steak of the fish world, everyone seems to love sea bass, particularly simply fried in butter. But the artichokes are the star of this dish. A scary thing the artichoke, in fact bit of a ballbreaker, but worth the effort. Follow this recipe and you'll be shocked at how good they are. But hey, we can't be scared of vegetables – can we?

SERVES 4

8 BABY GLOBE ARTICHOKES
1 LEMON, CUT IN HALF
2 TABLESPOONS VEGETABLE OIL, PLUS
   A SPLASH FOR COOKING THE FISH
1 SHALLOT, SLICED
1 CARROT, PEELED AND SLICED
1 CELERY STICK, SLICED
1 BAY LEAF
1 TEASPOON FENNEL SEEDS
1 TEASPOON CORIANDER SEEDS
SPRIG OF ROSEMARY
300ML WHITE WINE
50G BUTTER, PLUS A KNOB
250G DRAINED CANNED WHITE BEANS
   (CANNELLINI OR HARICOT)
4 X 150G PORTIONS SEA BASS FILLETS,
   SKIN ON
SALT AND FRESHLY GROUND BLACK PEPPER
KNOB OF BUTTER
8 SUN-DRIED TOMATO HALVES
8 BASIL LEAVES, SHREDDED

Peel the artichokes and rub them with the cut side of the lemon halves to stop them discolouring.

Heat the 2 tablespoons oil in a saucepan, add the shallot, carrot and celery and fry over a medium heat for 2 minutes.

Add the artichokes to the pan along with the bay leaf, fennel and coriander seeds and rosemary, then pour in the wine followed by 200ml cold water.

Simmer for about 10 minutes, or until the artichokes are tender.

Remove the artichokes from the pan. Scoop out and discard the choke in the centre of each with a teaspoon. then cut the artichokes in half. Set aside.

Pass the artichoke cooking liquid through a sieve into a saucepan, discarding the solids, and cook until reduced by half.

Whisk in the 50g butter, then add the beans and artichokes and warm through.

Heat the splash of vegetable oil in a frying pan over a medium heat, add the fish, skin-side down, and cook for 3 minutes. Turn the fish over and cook for a further 2 minutes. Season with salt and black pepper and finish with the knob of butter.

Stir the sun-dried tomatoes and basil into the beans and check the seasoning.

To serve, put the bean and artichoke pistou in a bowl and top with the fish.

TURBOT WITH SQUID ROLLED IN CRISPY PORK, APPLE +TARRAGON PUREE

Apple juice? Cooking in apple juice? Fish? Yes! Turbot is a big, meaty fish also known as bin lid, well the big ones are the shape and size of a bin lid. The apple juice doesn't penetrate the flesh; it cooks it and sticks to the outside, imparting just enough flavour so as not to overpower the fish. Together with the crispy squid and the sour apple purée, it's pure delight.

SERVES 4

½ TEASPOON GROUND GINGER
½ TEASPOON SWEET PAPRIKA
½ TEASPOON GARAM MASALA
100G PLAIN FLOUR
2 LARGE EGGS, BEATEN
120G SOSA AIR BAG FARINA (DRIED, POWDERED PORK SKIN, AVAILABLE FROM GOOD DELICATESSENS OR ONLINE)
8 X 200G SQUID TUBES, CLEANED AND CUT INTO RINGS
50G UNSALTED BUTTER
2 BRAMLEY APPLES, PEELED, CORED AND THINLY SLICED
500ML HOT CHICKEN STOCK
500ML APPLE JUICE
2 DRIED BAY LEAVES
4 SPRIGS OF THYME
VEGETABLE OIL, FOR DEEP-FRYING
2 SPRIGS OF TARRAGON
2 GRANNY SMITH APPLES
4 X 120G PORTIONS OF TURBOT FILLETS
SALT
WATERCRESS, TO GARNISH

Mix together the ground ginger, paprika and garam masala in a shallow bowl.

Put the flour in a second shallow bowl, the beaten eggs in a third bowl and the Air Bag in a fourth bowl.

Roll the squid rings first in the spice mix, next in the flour, then in the beaten eggs and finally in the Air Bag. Set aside until ready to fry.

Melt the butter in a saucepan, add the Bramley apple slices and gently cook down until soft.

Transfer the apple to a blender and whizz to a smooth purée, then pass through a sieve into a clean pan and set aside.

Meanwhile, pour the chicken stock and apple juice into a pan wide enough to poach the four turbot fillets. Add the bay leaves and thyme and bring to just below simmering point.

Heat the oil for deep-frying in a deep-fat fryer or deep saucepan until the temperature reaches 180°C.

Chop the tarragon, then peel, core and dice the Granny Smith apples. Set aside.

Gently poach the fish in the chicken stock and apple juice for 6–7 minutes, or until just cooked.

Add the diced apple and tarragon to the apple purée and gently heat up.

Deep-fry the squid, in batches, for about 1–2 minutes until golden brown and crispy. Remove from the oil and drain on kitchen paper, then season with a little salt.

Serve the poached turbot with a spoonful of the apple purée and the squid. Garnish with watercress.

ROAST SCALLOPS WITH PIPERADE + SCORCHED BABY GEM LETTUCE

Piperade, a spicy tomato-pepper sauce from the Basque region of France, can be used as a stewing ingredient or a garnish to a finished dish. This recipe uses a very small amount of granulated sugar to mellow out the sharp tang of the tomatoes and peppers.

2 GREEN PEPPERS
2 RED PEPPERS
2 ANAHEIM CHILLIES
2 TABLESPOONS EXTRA VIRGIN OLIVE OIL
150G BAYONNE HAM, DICED
1 LARGE SPANISH ONION, CHOPPED
2 GARLIC CLOVES, CRUSHED AND
    FINELY CHOPPED
½ TEASPOON SALT
¼ TEASPOON SWEET PAPRIKA
⅛ TEASPOON GROUND BLACK PEPPER
¼ TEASPOON GRANULATED SUGAR
410G CAN CHERRY TOMATOES, DICED
500G GREEN BEANS, TOPPED AND TAILED
5 BANANA SHALLOTS, FINELY DICED
ABOUT 400ML CLASSIC VINAIGRETTE
    (SEE PAGE 98), PLUS EXTRA TO SERVE
50ML SUNFLOWER OIL
9 SHELLED AND CLEANED SCALLOPS, ROES
    SEPARATED (SEE PAGE 80)
9 LITTLE GEM LETTUCE LEAVES
KNOB OF BUTTER

SERVES 3

Preheat the oven to 160°C/gas mark 3.

For the piperade, char the green and red peppers and chillies with a blowtorch until completely blackened all over. Put on a baking tray, loosely cover with foil and bake for 45 minutes until softened.

Remove the tray from the oven and leave the peppers and chillies to cool, then deseed and dice. Increase the oven temperature to 200°C/gas mark 6.

Heat the olive oil in a large saucepan over a medium heat, add the ham, onion and garlic and sauté for 5 minutes until the onion starts to soften.

Add the peppers and chillies, salt, paprika, black pepper and sugar and cook for 10 minutes, stirring occasionally, until the vegetables are cooked through.

Add the tomatoes to the cooked vegetables and simmer the mixture, uncovered, for 15 minutes until most of the liquid has evaporated and the sauce has thickened.

Blanch the green beans in a large saucepan of boiling water for about 2 minutes until they are soft but with a little bite. Drain immediately and refresh in iced water.

Sweat the shallots in a dry saucepan without oil very gently to remove the moisture.

In a separate pan, heat enough vinaigrette to cover the shallots, and once hot, pour over the shallots, then leave to cool.

Drain and dice the green beans, then add to the mixture to complete the green-bean vinaigrette.

Heat the sunflower oil in an ovenproof frying pan over a medium-high heat, and when hot, add the scallops and fry for 2 minutes until golden brown on the underside.

Add the roes, then place the pan in the oven for 3 minutes.

Meanwhile, scorch the lettuce leaves with the blowtorch.

Remove the pan from the oven to the hob, add the butter and quickly baste each scallop with it. Check that the scallops are golden brown and firm to the touch but not rubbery, then remove from the heat.

To serve, place three scallops on each plate with a spoonful of piperade, three scorched lettuce leaves and a drizzle of vinaigrette.

RED MULLET WITH CEPS +GOATS' CHEESE

Red mullet has a red, silky skin and a beautiful oil that seeps out when it is cooking. Ceps, the king of mushrooms, go fantastically with most things, but the mix of goats' cheese and red mullet is a true triumph. The combination works without the fish too. This is an autumnal dish that's like a warm but delicate marriage. Oh, the poetry! Said so softly by a big hairy man!

SERVES 2

½ SMALL PUMPKIN, SKIN ON, DESEEDED
KNOB OF BUTTER, PLUS EXTRA
    FOR BRUSHING
3 LARGE CEPS, CLEANED AND SLICED
3 LARGE HISPI CABBAGE LEAVES
    (SAVOY CABBAGE CAN ALSO BE USED)
SALT
100G GOATS' CHEESE, CRUMBLED
60G PUMPKIN SEEDS, TOASTED
FRESHLY GROUND BLACK PEPPER
VEGETABLE OIL, FOR DEEP-FRYING
1 MEDIUM RED MULLET, FILLETED
    AND PIN-BONED
SPLASH OF RAPESEED OIL

Preheat the oven to 180°C/gas mark 4.

Put the pumpkin on a baking tray and bake for 35 minutes until tender.

Melt the butter in a frying pan, add the ceps and cook over a high heat for 5 minutes.

Blanch two of the cabbage leaves in a large saucepan of salted boiling water for 1 minute. Drain the leaves and refresh in iced water.

Cut away the bottom of the stem from the cabbage leaves, ensuring that the leaves remain whole. Place the ceps on one side of the leaves, then sprinkle the ceps with the goats' cheese and pumpkin seeds.

Slice the roasted pumpkin and remove the skin, then lay the pieces on top of the cheese, then season with salt and black pepper. Fold each leaf over to cover the filling and brush the outside with butter.

Heat the oil for deep-frying in a deep-fat fryer or deep saucepan until the temperature reaches 180°C (use a food thermometer).

Put the stuffed leaves on a baking tray and bake for 6 minutes.

Rub the mullet fillets with the rapeseed oil and bake on a separate baking tray for 6 minutes.

Shred the remaining cabbage leaf and deep-fry for 30–40 seconds, then remove from the oil, drain on kitchen paper and season with salt and black pepper.

To serve, place a stuffed cabbage on each plate. Season the fish and place alongside. Garnish with the deep-fried shredded cabbage.

SCALLOPS WITH RAW VEGETABLES, ALMOND SATAY + PONZU

Scallops go with everything. Here, I've paired them with the citrusy Japanese sauce ponzu, which sounds like a cowboy that lives in a puddle. Anyway, changing peanuts for almonds gives a more delicate and rounder flavour, and the umami of the ponzu gives it a kick like that of an eight-year-old Spanish donkey. ¡Ay caramba!

SERVES 4

4 LARGE SCALLOPS IN THEIR SHELLS
50ML SUNFLOWER OIL
KNOB OF BUTTER
1 LIME, CUT IN HALF, FOR SQUEEZING
A FEW CORIANDER SHOOTS OR SPRIGS
   OF CORIANDER, TO GARNISH

FOR THE VEGETABLES
50G BEANSPROUTS
50G MANGETOUT, FINELY SLICED
   INTO STICKS
50G CARROT, PEELED AND FINELY SLICED
   INTO STICKS

FOR THE PONZU DRESSING
2 TABLESPOONS DASHI STOCK
1 TABLESPOON STOCK SYRUP
   (SEE PAGE 143)
1 TABLESPOON RICE WINE VINEGAR
½ TABLESPOON FISH SAUCE
3 TABLESPOONS FRESHLY SQUEEZED
   LEMON JUICE
50ML SOY SAUCE

FOR THE ALMOND SATAY
15G BUTTER
1 TABLESPOON VEGETABLE OIL
2 SHALLOTS, FINELY CHOPPED
1½ GARLIC CLOVES, FINELY CHOPPED
60G FRESH GINGER, PEELED AND
   FINELY GRATED
300G BLANCHED ALMONDS, TOASTED
   AND CHOPPED
2 TABLESPOONS RUNNY HONEY
75ML SOY SAUCE
JUICE OF 1 LIME
1 RED CHILLI, FINELY CHOPPED
A SMALL HANDFUL OF CORIANDER LEAVES,
   FINELY CHOPPED

Mix the vegetables together and set aside.

Mix all the ponzu dressing ingredients together in a bowl and set aside.

For the satay, melt the butter with the oil in a saucepan, add the shallots and garlic and cook gently until softened but not coloured. Add the ginger and continue to sweat for 5 minutes.

Stir in the almonds, honey, soy sauce and lime juice, and cook for 2 minutes.

Remove from the heat and add the chilli and the coriander.

Preheat the oven to 200°C/gas mark 6.

To prepare the scallops, hold with the top flat shell uppermost, insert a blunt knife between the shells near the hinge and prise the shells open. Insert the knife and release the scallop from the bottom shell, then open the shell fully. Remove and discard the frill around the outside of the scallop and carefully cut away the black stomach sac. Pull off any discoloured parts around the white flesh. Rinse the scallops thoroughly under cold running water. Separate the roe (coral) from the white flesh and set aside.

Wash and dry the scallop shells and set aside for serving.

Heat the oil in an ovenproof frying pan over a medium-high heat, and when hot, add the scallops and fry for 2 minutes until golden brown on the underside.

Turn the scallops over and fry for a further minute. Add the roes, then place the pan in the oven for 3 minutes.

Remove the pan from the oven to the hob, add the butter and quickly baste each scallop with it, then finish with a squeeze of lime juice. Check that the scallops are golden brown and firm to the touch but not rubbery, then remove from the heat.

Put the scallops in the reserved shells with the raw vegetables, pour over a spoonful of warm almond satay, then 3 tablespoons of the ponzu dressing. Arrange a few coriander shoots or sprigs over the top and serve.

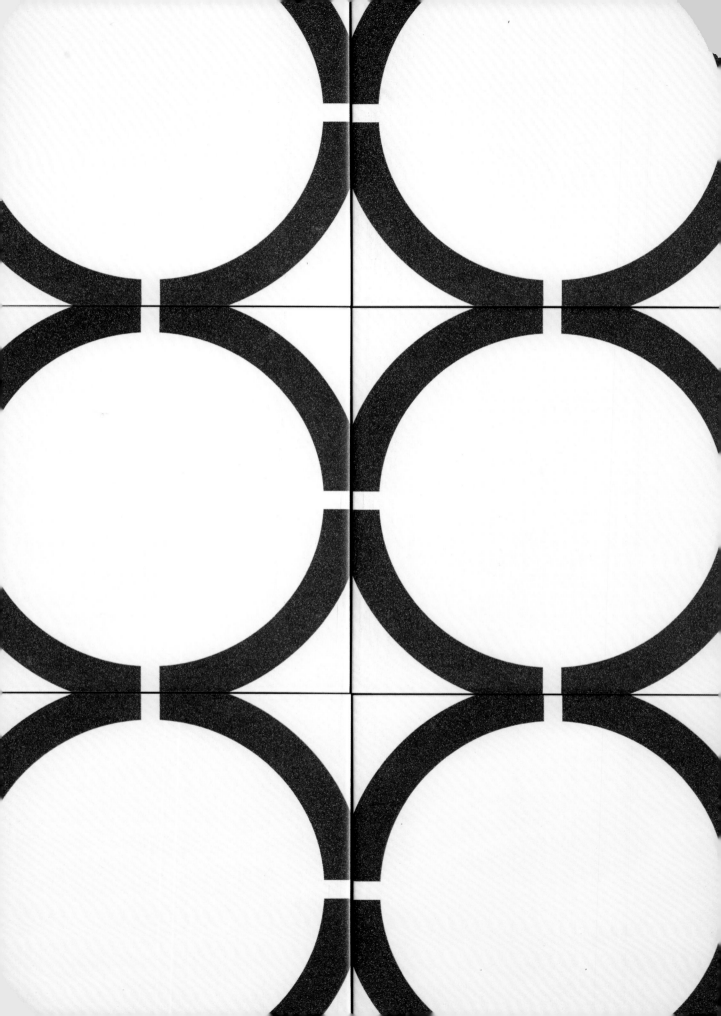

this little piggy
went to market

Who ate the pork?

Food at home was precious, always homemade and treated with a lot of respect. Every portion was accounted for.

Every Sunday we had a roast lunch – juicy meat with crispy potatoes, two veg and gravy. My favourite day, and my favourite meal. But the best part of Sunday was teatime or, if you're posh, supper. It would be pikelets, scones, malt bread and, if we were lucky, leftover roast meat sandwiches with stuffing. What a treat!

One Sunday, there was leftover pork on the bone. It sat on the side ready to be carved and served on heavily buttered bread.

I was playing in my room and my brother came in, looking a little sheepish.

'What you up to?' I asked.

'Nothing,' he said, wiping his mouth and turning a delicate shade of red.

Then I heard shouting from downstairs. It was Mom, berating my dad.

'You've eaten the meat, you greedy beggar!'

My dad, like he did every Sunday, was having a little nap, digesting his lunch and the pre-lunch pint he'd had down the local pub, The Cent.

My dad woke up just as Mom was wrapping the newspaper around his head.

'No I never!'

A meeting was then called and interrogations began. 'Who ate the pork?' Followed by 'Who ate the pork?' We all said that it wasn't us, but in the end my brother was rumbled. Stern words were said. The punishment was bread and water, then bed. Lesson learnt. Big time!

ROAST CHICKEN THIGHS WITH MORTADELLA SAUSAGE, FETA + BLACK OLIVES

As I have said before, the thighs are the best part of a bird. Oh, and the wings! Love eating meat off the bone. Love rolling up my sleeves, picking it up and gnawing away. As children, my brothers and sisters – Gaynor, Gareth and Gemma – and I would take it in turns every Sunday to pick at the carcass of the roast. Every scrap, until it ended up looking like a cartoon skeleton.

SPLASH OF VEGETABLE OIL
8 CHICKEN THIGHS, SKIN ON, BONED
1 SHALLOT, CHOPPED
1 GARLIC CLOVE, CHOPPED
300G MORTADELLA SAUSAGE, DICED
100ML SWEET WHITE WINE
100ML HOT BROWN CHICKEN STOCK
  (SEE PAGE 184)
3 TABLESPOONS CHOPPED PITTED
  BLACK OLIVES
300G FETA CHEESE, DICED
½ TABLESPOON CHOPPED TARRAGON
½ TABLESPOON CHOPPED PARSLEY
SALT AND FRESHLY GROUND BLACK PEPPER
50ML DOUBLE CREAM

SERVES 4

Preheat the oven to 180°C/gas mark 4.

Heat the oil in a flameproof casserole dish, add the chicken thighs and cook until browned and sealed on all sides. Remove from the dish and set aside.

Add the shallot and garlic to the dish and sweat over a gentle heat until lightly coloured.

Add the sausage, then the white wine and simmer until reduced by half.

Return the chicken thighs to the dish and cover with the chicken stock. Put the lid on the dish and place in the oven for 10–15 minutes until the chicken is cooked through.

Remove the dish from the oven, stir in the olives, feta and herbs and season with salt and pepper. Finally, add the cream. Serve with pasta or seasonal potatoes.

CHICKEN SUPREME +POMEGRANATE COUSCOUS

Poaching chicken is nice. Roasting it is better. Doing both is the business. The harissa adds a little heat and the lightly spiced, fruited couscous complexity to what might otherwise be a boring meat. Couscous with fruit, isn't my favourite but Phil my sous chef changed my mind. (Not like that - I still like the ladies. And to put the record straight Phil is married. Happily married. Enough said. Line drawn). This couscous also goes well with fish or as a vegetarian dish.

SERVES 4

FOR THE CHICKEN
600ML CHICKEN STOCK
25G BUTTER
4 BONELESS CHICKEN BREAST, SKIN ON
SPLASH OF VEGETABLE OIL
2 ONIONS, THINLY SLICED
2 GARLIC CLOVES, ROUGHLY CHOPPED
SALT
4 RED PEPPERS, FINELY CHOPPED
2KG RIPE TOMATOES, CHOPPED
20G HARISSA
40ML MALT VINEGAR
½ TEASPOON XANTHAN GUM
FRESHLY GROUND BLACK PEPPER

FOR THE COUSCOUS
25G SALTED BUTTER
1 RED ONION, DICED
1 TEASPOON RAS EL HANOUT
250ML HOT CHICKEN STOCK
250G COUSCOUS
40G RAISINS
40G READY-TO-EAT DRIED APRICOTS,
   CHOPPED
40G MEDJOOL DATES, CHOPPED
SEEDS FROM 1 POMEGRANATE
1 TABLESPOON PUMPKIN SEEDS
1 TABLESPOON FLAKED ALMONDS
1 ORANGE, SEGMENTED

TO SERVE
3 TABLESPOONS HARISSA
3 TEASPOONS HERB OIL
2 CHICORY (ENDIVE) LEAVES, SPLIT IN HALF
2 TABLESPOONS CLASSIC VINAIGRETTE
   (SEE PAGE 98)
A FEW SPRIGS OF CORIANDER

Preheat the oven to 200°C/gas mark 6.

Pour the stock into an ovenproof sauté pan and bring to a gentle simmer. Add the butter and chicken, cover with a lid and place in the oven for 12–15 minutes until the chicken is cooked through. Remove from the oven, lift the chicken out and pat dry.

Pour off any cooking liquid and put the pan over a medium-high heat. Add the chicken breast, skin-side down, and cook until the skin is caramelised. Leave to rest.

Heat the oil in a large pan and sweat the onions and garlic over a gentle heat until softened, seasoning with a small amount of salt to help break them down.

Add the peppers and tomatoes and cook, stirring, for 2–3 minutes. Add a splash of water, cover the pan with a tight fitting a lid and gently simmer over a low heat for 10 minutes. Remove the clingfilm and cook the mixture until reduced and thickened.

Pour into a blender, add the harissa, vinegar and xanthan gum and whizz on a high speed until smooth. Pass through a sieve and season to taste.

For the couscous: Put the butter, onion and ras el hanout in a saucepan over a medium heat and cook for 3 minutes without colouring. Add the chicken stock and bring to the boil.

Meanwhile, put the couscous in a large bowl. Pour over the boiling stock and immediately cover the bowl with clingfilm. Leave to stand for 5 minutes, or until the couscous has absorbed all the stock. Stir the couscous with a fork, ensuring that any clumps are broken up. Add all the remaining ingredients and mix well.

To serve: Swipe the harissa in the centre of each plate.

Carve the chicken into thirds and season with salt and black pepper, then place off-centre of the harissa. Flick the herb oil over the harissa.

Dress the chicory with the vinaigrette, season and stand the leaves up against the chicken breast.

Finish with the coriander and serve immediately, along with a bowl of the pomegranate couscous.

POMEGRANATE
COUSCOUS

SWEET + SOUR BUNNY

Rabbit is fantastic meat; it's tasty and low in fat. The legs are great. You can roast them, but the lack of fat means they can go dry easily. Braising them is a better cooking method, especially if you then roll them in a sticky aromatic sweet and sour glaze. It will make you forget all about Bugs Bunny and Watership Down.

SPLASH OF VEGETABLE OIL
4 RABBIT LEGS
300ML HOT CHICKEN STOCK
1 VANILLA POD, SPLIT LENGTHWAYS
1 CARDAMOM POD
1 GARLIC CLOVE, PEELED
½ TABLESPOON CORIANDER SEEDS
6 BLACK PEPPERCORNS

FOR THE SWEET AND SOUR SAUCE

150ML MALT VINEGAR
150G CASTER SUGAR
2 TABLESPOON SOY SAUCE
1 SMALL RED CHILLI, CHOPPED
1 TABLESPOON GRATED FRESH GINGER
1 TABLESPOON TAMARIND PASTE
2 STAR ANISE
¼ PINEAPPLE, SKIN, EYES AND CORE
    REMOVED, THEN DICED

TO GARNISH

1 RED CHILLI, FINELY CHOPPED
2 TABLESPOONS CHOPPED CORIANDER
ZEST OF ½ LIME

Preheat the oven to 180°C/gas mark 4.

Heat the oil in a flameproof casserole dish, add the rabbit legs and cook until golden brown and sealed on all sides. Remove from the dish.

Add the stock to the dish and deglaze, scraping up all the sediment with a wooden spoon.

Stir in the split vanilla pod, cardamom, garlic, coriander seeds and black peppercorns, then add the rabbit legs to the stock.

Cover the dish and place in the oven for 25 minutes, or until the rabbit is tender.

Remove the legs and set aside. Strain the cooking liquid through a sieve into a saucepan and cook on the hob until reduced by half.

To make the sauce, put the vinegar and sugar in a saucepan and heat over a medium heat to a light caramel colour.

Add the soy sauce, chilli, ginger, tamarind paste, star anise and pineapple and cook for a further 2 minutes.

Stir in the reduced rabbit stock and cook for another 2 minutes.

Add the rabbit legs to the pan and turn them in the sauce to glaze them. Lift the legs out, place in a serving dish and pour over the sauce. Sprinkle with the chopped chilli and coriander for garnish, and finish with the lime zest. Serve with steamed jasmine rice or cooked noodles with sesame seeds.

SERVES 4

DUCK WITH SPICED PLUM JAM + WATERCRESS

Big, juicy, spicy plums! Oo-er missus! They're exactly what you need to cut through the rich duck. The crisp pak choi blends and adds balance. Duck is a fab meat either spiced up or classically served. Fat and delicious!

SERVES 4

2 HEADS OF PAK CHOI
3 DUCK BREASTS
SALT AND FRESHLY GROUND BLACK PEPPER
A BUNCH OF WATERCRESS, TO GARNISH

FOR THE PLUM JAM
200G CASTER SUGAR
200ML WHITE WINE VINEGAR
1 MEDIUM CHILLI, CHOPPED
PINCH OF CHILLI POWDER
2 GARLIC CLOVES, SLICED
SQUEEZE OF LIME JUICE
SPLASH OF SOY SAUCE
6 PLUMS, STONED AND CHOPPED
1 TABLESPOON CHOPPED CORIANDER
SALT AND GROUND GINGER

Preheat the oven to 180°C/gas mark 4.

For the plum jam, heat the sugar and vinegar in a saucepan, stirring until the sugar has dissolved, then cook until the mixture starts to thicken.

Add the chilli and chilli powder, garlic, lime juice and soy sauce, then stir in the plums and cook for 20–30 minutes until tender.

Add the coriander, then remove the pan from the heat and season with salt and ground ginger.

Break the pak choi into individual leaves, then split each leaf down its length. Set aside.

Prepare the duck breasts by removing any sinew from the underside of the breast and using a very sharp knife to score the skin with a series of slashes, being careful not to go too deeply and cut into the flesh.

Heat a frying pan over a medium heat, add the breasts, skin-side down, and cook for about 3 minutes until the skin has caramelised. Pour off the excess fat and reserve.

Lay the duck breasts, skin-side down, in a roasting tin and place in the oven for 7–8 minutes. Remove from the oven and leave to rest for 10 minutes.

Pour the reserved fat and any in the roasting tin back into the frying pan and set over a medium heat. Once hot, add the pak choi and toss in the hot duck fat. Remove from the pan and season with salt and black pepper.

Carve the duck into slices and divide between four plates, then serve with the pak choi and plum jam, garnished with watercress.

SPICED PORK BELLY WITH GRILLED PAK CHOI

When I think of pork belly, I think of roast with mash and vegetables, which is cool and one of my favourite meals. It reminds me of home and family dinners. This method of cooking belly is really organised, which is great if you want to do it a day in advance. Prepped, cooked and pressed with the spices, it's perfect for a dinner party or a casual soirée – depending on your jacket and the cut of your jib, of course. Grilling the Chinese veg also makes a great change to a stir-fry. When I walk around the Chinese quarter and see the ducks and bellies hanging in the windows, it makes my mouth water. So here is my take on Chinese pork belly.

SERVES 4

½ PORK BELLY (ABOUT 500G), BONED
75ML DARK SOY SAUCE
½ TABLESPOON CORIANDER SEEDS
½ TABLESPOON GROUND BLACK PEPPER
50ML FISH SAUCE
50ML MIRIN
5 STAR ANISE
1 VANILLA POD, SPLIT LENGTHWAYS
½ FRESH GINGER ROOT (ABOUT 200G), PEELED
3 GREEN CHILLIES
3 CARDAMOM PODS
500 ML HOT CHICKEN STOCK
½ GARLIC BULB
SPLASH OF VEGETABLE OIL

FOR THE GRILLED PAK CHOI
25ML SESAME OIL
2 LARGE HEADS OF PAK CHOI, CUT IN HALF LENGTHWAYS
2 TABLESPOONS SESAME SEEDS, TOASTED
1 TABLESPOON POPPY SEEDS, TOASTED

Preheat the oven to 180°C/gas mark 4.

Lay the pork belly in a deep roasting tin. Add all the remaining ingredients, except the oil, pour over 500ml cold water and cover with foil. Place in the oven for 2½ hours, or until the pork is tender.

Remove the roasting tin from the oven and leave the pork belly to cool for 20 minutes.

Remove the pork belly from the cooking liquid and wrap in clingfilm. Transfer the pork to a clean tray and press down to flatten.

Pass the cooking liquid through a sieve into a saucepan, then cook until reduced to a coating consistency.

Cut the pork into squares about 120g in weight.

Heat an ovenproof frying pan over a medium–high heat, add the oil and pan-fry the squares on each side until golden.

Place the pan in the oven, still at 180°C/gas mark 4, for 4–5 minutes.

Meanwhile, heat a separate frying pan over a medium heat, add the sesame oil and then the pak choi, cut-sides down, and cook until golden. Turn over and cook for a further minute, then dress the leaves with mixed sesame and poppy seeds.

To serve, remove the pork from the oven, glaze with the reduced cooking liquid and serve with the grilled pak choi.

CONFIT LEMON +VANILLA PORK BELLY +SALT-BAKED PINEAPPLE

The question you maybe asking is 'Why confit?', which means to cook submerged in fat. Well, no fat, no flavour, as they say. Confit-ing softens the meat. Then it's scorched with a blowtorch, which caramelises it. Mmm ... I need a tissue, I'm dribbling. Baking the pineapple in salt gives it a sweet but salty flavour that cuts through the fat of the pork.

2.5 LITRES SUNFLOWER OIL
1 GARLIC BULB, CUT IN HALF LENGTHWAYS
2 SPRIGS OF THYME
3 BAY LEAVES
8 CARDAMOM PODS, CRUSHED
1 LEMON, PEEL REMOVED WITH A PEELER, THEN JUICED
2 VANILLA PODS, SPLIT LENGTHWAYS
2KG PIECE OF BONELESS PORK BELLY

Preheat the oven to 150°C/gas mark 2.

Put the oil, garlic, herbs, cardamom pods, lemon peel and juice in a roasting tin. Scrape in the seeds from the vanilla pods, then whisk everything together to evenly distribute them.

Add the pork belly, ensuring that it is fully submerged in the oil mixture.

Put the roasting tin on the hob over a medium heat to warm the oil for about 5 minutes, but be careful not to begin frying the pork. Cover the roasting tin with foil and roast the pork belly for about 3 hours.

Remove the tin from the oven and lift off the foil. Test that the pork belly is tender enough by inserting a small knife – there should be little or no resistance. If there is still some resistance, cover with a fresh piece of foil and roast for a further 30 minutes.

Once cooked, remove the tin from the oven and leave the pork to rest in the oil for 15 minutes.

Carefully lift the pork from the oil and place it on a flat baking tray.

To crisp the skin, place the pork under a hot grill until coloured, being careful not to burn the skin. Alternatively, use a blowtorch, like we do in the restaurant.

Carve the pork and arrange on individual plates with the sliced Salt-baked Pineapple (see below).

SERVES 4–6

FOR THE SALT-BAKED PINEAPPLE
500G CLEAN, LARGE-GRAINED INDUSTRIAL WHITE ROCK SALT
500ML EGG WHITES (LEFT OVER FROM MAKING ICE CREAM OR CREME BRULEE – SEE PAGES 138 AND 119), BEATEN
½ PINEAPPLE, HALVED LENGTHWAYS, SKIN ON

TO SERVE
CLASSIC VINAIGRETTE (SEE PAGE 98)
GROUND GINGER

Preheat the oven to 180°C/gas mark 4.

Mix together the salt and egg whites so that you have a mixture with the texture of wet sand.

Put the pineapple, skin-side up, in a large casserole dish or roasting tin and cover with the salt mixture, ensuring that you pack it firmly around the pineapple.

Bake the pineapple for 45 minutes to an hour. Remove from the oven and leave to cool.

Gently break the salt casing and remove the pineapple. Using a sharp knife, peel the pineapple and cut into large slices.

Dress with vinaigrette and ground ginger and serve with the pork belly.

CONFIT LEMON + VANILLA
PORK BELLY WITH
SALT-BAKED PINEAPPLE

ROAST DUCK BREASTS WITH GOATS' CURD + ELDERFLOWER, PEAS + RADISHES

Elderflower and goat's cheese are a lovely sweet and sour pairing. If you can make your own cordial, that's great, though lots of the flowers smell like wee, even if they don't taste like it. Roasting the duck nice and pink, rendering the fat, then serving it with the cool fresh goats' cheese and elderflower gives you a temperature change and the acidic sweet flavours all work jolly well!

SERVES 2

2 DUCK BREASTS
75ML WHITE WINE
SPRIG OF THYME
1 BAY LEAF
KNOB OF BUTTER
100ML PEKING DUCK SAUCE
100G GOATS' CURD
20ML ELDERFLOWER CORDIAL
SALT AND FRESHLY GROUND
   BLACK PEPPER
150G FRESH PEAS
3 MINT LEAVES, FINELY SLICED
200ML CLASSIC VINAIGRETTE (SEE
   PAGE 98)
FRESHLY GROUND BLACK PEPPER
5 RADISHES, HALVED
A HANDFUL OF PEA SHOOTS
FRESHLY GROUND BLACK PEPPER

Preheat the oven to 200°C/gas mark 6.

Prepare the duck breasts by removing any sinew from the underside of the breast and using a very sharp knife to score the skin with a series of slashes, being careful not to go too deeply and cut into the flesh.

Put the duck breasts, skin-side down, in a cold ovenproof frying pan over a medium heat and cook gently to render the fat. Once the fat starts to caramelise, place the pan in the oven for 6–8 minutes, or until the duck is cooked to your liking.

Remove the pan from the oven, lift the duck out and leave to rest.

Deglaze the pan with the white wine, scraping up all the sediment with a wooden spoon, then add the thyme and bay leaf.

Cook until most of the wine has evaporated, then whisk in the butter and duck sauce, pass through a fine strainer into a separate pan and set aside.

Beat the goats' curd in a bowl with the elderflower cordial and season with salt.

In a separate bowl, mix the peas with the mint and a little of the vinaigrette. Season with salt.

Dress the radishes with the vinaigrette and season with salt.

To serve, spoon the goats' curd onto each plate, then spoon the peas around, lay over the radishes and finish with the pea shoots and a twist of black pepper over the goats' curd. Check that the temperature of the duck breast is hot enough and heat the sauce through. Season and carve the duck, then serve on the plates with the sauce on the side.

PURNELL'S PEKING DUCK

I wanted to do Peking duck so I read and studied a few recipes and came up with my own one. It's great if you just want to cook breasts (Mmmmmm breasts). Marinate for 4 hours, then roast with some raw veg and ponzu (see page 80). Use the garnish from the scallop dish. Is it Peking duck or just looking around the corner? No, no, no, what a poor joke. I'm so sorry.

4 DUCK BREASTS
135G RUNNY HONEY
30G DARK SOY SAUCE
30G BROWN SUGAR
30G CHINESE FIVE-SPICE POWDER

SERVES 4

Prepare the duck breasts by removing any sinew from the underside of the breast and using a very sharp knife to score the skin with a series of slashes, being careful not to go too deeply and cut into the flesh.

Mix together the honey, soy sauce, sugar, five-spice powder and 60ml cold water in a large bowl. Add the duck, turning to coat, cover the bowl with clingfilm and leave to marinate in the fridge for 5 hours.

Preheat the oven to 180°C/gas mark 4. Remove the duck breasts from the marinade and rinse off any excess.

Place the duck breasts in a roasting tray and roast in the oven for 10–12 minutes, until cooked.

Slice the duck thinly and serve with salad or spicy noodles.

CARAMELISED, SLOW-COOKED LAMB

Shoulder of lamb, with its layers of fat, is so tasty that cooking it slowly on the bone is the only way to go. Rubbing in some spices, then colouring it with brown sugar puts it on another level entirely. Finishing by putting it under the grill is fine, but if you get to use a blowtorch it's mega. Like Arnie or Sly Stallone in an action movie. You'll be back!

SERVES 4–6

FOR THE LAMB
1 TABLESPOON GROUND CUMIN
1 TABLESPOON GROUND GINGER
1 TEASPOON DRIED CHILLI FLAKES
½ TABLESPOON GARAM MASALA
½ TABLESPOON GROUND CINNAMON
1 SHOULDER OF LAMB ON THE BONE,
    ABOUT 1.8KG
2 GARLIC BULBS, SEPARATED INTO
    CLOVES, UNPEELED
2 ONIONS, QUARTERED
20G FRESH ROSEMARY
25G LIGHT SOFT BROWN SUGAR

FOR THE CLASSIC VINAIGRETTE
200ML SUNFLOWER OIL
50ML WHITE WINE VINEGAR
1 TEASPOON DIJON MUSTARD

FOR THE GREEN VEGETABLES
2 HEADS OF LITTLE GEM LETTUCE
50G BABY SPINACH
SALT
200G FINE GREEN BEANS
300G PEAS
200G MANGETOUT
50G WATERCRESS

Mix all the spices together and rub all over the lamb in a dish. Cover and leave in the fridge overnight so that the lamb takes on all the flavour of the spices.

Preheat the oven to 180°C/gas mark 4. Remove the lamb from the fridge and allow it to return to room temperature.

Put the garlic and onions into a roasting tin with the rosemary and place the lamb on top. Roast for 2–2½ hours, or until the lamb is cooked through and very tender.

While the lamb is roasting, prepare the vinaigrette by whisking together the oil, vinegar and mustard in a bowl.

Separate the leaves of the little gem lettuce and put in a bowl with the spinach leaves.

Bring a pan of salted water to the boil. Top and tail the green beans, then drop them into the boiling water. After 2 minutes, add the peas and mangetout and boil for a further minute.

Drain the vegetables and immediately add to the bowl with the lettuce and spinach. Add the watercress and dress all the leaves and vegetables with the vinaigrette.

When the lamb is ready, remove it from the oven and leave it to rest for 15 minutes.

Once rested, sprinkle the fat side of the lamb with the sugar. Caramelise the sugar and fat with a blowtorch or by placing under a hot grill.

Carve the lamb and serve with the dressed leaves and vegetables.

ROAST RACK OF LAMB WITH ORANGE + FENUGREEK-GLAZED CHICORY

Endive, or chicory as it's also known, is bitter but with a great texture, and when cooked with citrus and sugar it's transformed into an amazing vegetable. Fenugreek is great with both fish and meat, and adds spice and complexity to this dish. The rack of lamb is a 'rare' (no pun intended) treat – juicy, fatty, tender and indulgent. It's enough to leave any Hannibal Lecter drooling. Just grab a bottle of Chianti and some fava beans, but maybe drop the mask.

SERVES 4

8-BONE RACK OF LAMB, FRENCH TRIMMED
2 SPRIGS OF ROSEMARY
1 GARLIC CLOVE
2 HEADS OF CHICORY (ENDIVE),
    CUT IN HALF
50G BROWN SUGAR
300ML FRESH ORANGE JUICE
1 BAY LEAF
1 TABLESPOON FENUGREEK SEEDS
SPRIG OF MARJORAM, LEAVES PICKED

Preheat the oven to 180°C/gas mark 4.

Heat a large ovenproof frying pan over a medium-high heat, add the rack of lamb, fat-side down, and cook until golden brown. Then brown and seal all sides of the lamb, draining any excess fat from the pan.

Add the rosemary and garlic to the pan and place in the oven for 14–16 minutes.

Remove the pan from the oven, lift the lamb out of the pan onto a platter and leave to rest for 15 minutes.

While the lamb is resting, put the frying pan on the hob over a medium-high heat, add the chicory, cut-side down, and cook until browned, then add the sugar, orange juice, bay leaf and fenugreek seeds. Cook for 1 minute until the sugar has dissolved then place in the oven for 1 minute until cooked.

Remove the pan from the oven, lift the chicory out and set aside, then reduce the cooking liquid in the pan on the hob to a glaze.

Carve the lamb into cutlets and place on plates. Lay the chicory alongside and cover with the glaze, then sprinkle with the marjoram leaves.

RACK OF LAMB IS PARTICULARLY DELICIOUS, BUT IF YOU PREFER YOU CAN ALSO USE LAMB STEAKS.

PIGS' CHEEKS WITH APPLE PUREE, CRISPY PORK, HISPI CABBAGE + LETTUCE

Cheeks. Yes, the ones on a pig's face. Imagine trying to serve a pig's bum. That would be some portion! This is a really popular dish – tender and a little sweet the way I cook it – but people can be put off by the idea that they're eating a pig's face. So don't tell them until after they've eaten it.

FOR THE PIGS' CHEEKS
1 HEAD OF CELERY, ROUGHLY CHOPPED
3 ONIONS, ROUGHLY CHOPPED
4 CARROTS, PEELED AND ROUGHLY CHOPPED
1 GARLIC BULB, CLOVES SEPARATED, PEELED AND ROUGHLY CHOPPED
20 PIGS' CHEEKS
½ BUNCH OF THYME
80G BLACK TREACLE
1 TEASPOON CRACKED BLACK PEPPER
SALT AND FRESHLY GROUND BLACK PEPPER
2 TABLESPOONS CORNFLOUR OR POTATO STARCH (FECULE)

FOR THE APPLE PUREE
100G SALTED BUTTER
2 BRAMLEY APPLES, PEELED, CORED AND THINLY SLICED
SALT AND GROUND GINGER

FOR THE CRISPY PORK
SUNFLOWER OIL, FOR DEEP-FRYING
300G SOSA AIR BAG FARINA (SEE PAGE 76)

FOR THE GREENS
1 HEAD OF HISPI CABBAGE
1 ICEBERG LETTUCE

TO SERVE
CAPERS
PICKLED SHALLOTS
1 GRANNY SMITH APPLE (FROZEN FOR 24 HOURS)

Preheat the oven to 170°C/gas mark 3.

For the pigs' cheeks, put the vegetables, garlic, cheeks and thyme into a very deep roasting tin. Pour in enough cold water to completely submerge, then add the treacle and black pepper. Cover with two layers of foil and place in the oven for 3 hours.

Remove the tin from the oven and check that a knife easily goes through the cheeks. If there is any resistance, re-cover the tin and return to the oven until the cheeks are soft enough for a knife to easily pass through them. Once cooked, remove the tin from the oven and leave the cheeks to cool.

Peel and discard the fat from the cheeks, then place them on a tray, cover the tray with clingfilm and refrigerate until required.

Pass the cooking liquid through a sieve into a saucepan and cook until reduced to about 1 litre, then season with salt and black pepper.

Mix the cornflour or potato starch with a little cold water to make a paste, stir into the liquid and cook until thickened so that it coats the back of a spoon. Strain again and set aside.

For the apple purée: Melt the butter in a saucepan and sweat the apples over a medium heat until they start to go mushy. Stir in 100ml cold water, cover the pan and leave to cook over a medium heat for 5 minutes. Remove the clingfilm and cook the mixture to a thick purée.

Transfer the apple to a blender and whizz until smooth, then pass through a sieve and season with salt and ground ginger. Set aside.

For the crispy pork: heat the oil for deep-frying in a deep-fat fryer or deep saucepan until the temperature reaches 180°C. Deep-fry the Air Bag for 1 minute, stirring constantly to ensure that it is evenly crispy. Remove from the oil and drain on kitchen paper.

For the greens: remove and discard the darker leaves from the cabbage and lettuce. Separate the remaining leaves and cut into 10cm diamond-shaped pieces. Wash and drain well, keeping the cabbage and lettuce separate.

Sprinkle the pigs' cheeks with capers, pickled shallots and the crispy Air Bag. Serve with the cabbage, lettuce and apple purée, grating the frozen apple over the top to finish.

SERVES 4-6

RUMP STEAK WITH BAKED POTATO GRATIN

Everyone loves steak, well except vegetarians. And steak and chips is like a horse and carriage, apples and pears – no, wait, that's rhyming slang for stairs. What am I saying? Oh yes, chips! They're great with steak, but why not try something different, like my baked potato gratin? It's baked potato in a mash, with the gratined skin – nothing is wasted and it tastes amazing. Also, no deep-fat fryer! Plus you can make small individual portions or one great big one.

SERVES 4

200G CLEAN, LARGE-GRAINED INDUSTRIAL WHITE ROCK SALT
2 LARGE BAKING POTATOES, SKIN ON, WASHED
300ML DOUBLE CREAM
1 GARLIC CLOVE
A BUNCH OF ROSEMARY
SALT AND CRACKED BLACK PEPPER
300G FIRM MATURE CHEDDAR CHEESE, GRATED
4 X 200G RUMP STEAKS, FAT ON
SPLASH OF VEGETABLE OIL
10G BUTTER

Preheat the oven to 180°C/gas mark 4.

Sprinkle the salt onto a baking tray and place the potatoes on top.

Bake the potatoes for about 1½ hours, or until they are soft.

While the potatoes are baking, heat the cream with the garlic and rosemary in a saucepan and bring to the boil. Remove the pan from the heat and leave to infuse.

Remove the potatoes from the oven and leave to cool.

Cut the potatoes in half and scoop out the potato, reserving the skins. Pass the potato through a fine sieve into a mixing bowl.

Strain the garlic and rosemary from the infused cream and fold into the potato, season to taste with salt and cracked black pepper and divide the creamed potatoes between four ramekins.

Shred the potato skins and sprinkle over the creamed potato in the ramekins. Top with the grated cheese and bake for 15 minutes.

Meanwhile, heat a frying pan over a high heat. After 7 minutes, add the steaks to the hot pan with the oil and cook for 2 minutes, then turn over and cook for a further 2 minutes.

Add the butter to the pan and baste the steaks with it. Remove from the pan and leave to rest for 5 minutes.

To serve, place a ramekin with the gratin on each plate. Season the steaks with salt and black pepper and serve alongside. Finish with a green crispy salad.

50/50 BURGER

50/50 means half beef, half pork – the pork fat makes it so tasty. Again, I've said it once and I'll say it again – make your own (this is getting tedious)! Together with the bone marrow, spice and a gooey cheesy top, this makes for a mega burger. It would smash that clown and king to bits!

SERVES 4

FOR THE BURGERS
250G STEAK MINCE
250G FATTY PORK MINCE
60ML WORCESTERSHIRE SAUCE
SCANT TEASPOON TABASCO SAUCE
80G BONE MARROW, DICED
10G SALT

FOR THE BLACK PEPPER GLAZE
500ML MALT VINEGAR
250G CASTER SUGAR
125ML SOY SAUCE
2 TEASPOONS MARMITE

FOR MONTGOMERY CHEESE SLICE
275ML FULL-FAT MILK
500G MONTGOMERY'S MATURE CHEDDAR, CHOPPED
65G PLAIN FLOUR
65G FRESH WHITE BREADCRUMBS
SALT
1 MEDIUM EGG
1 MEDIUM EGG YOLK
1 TABLESPOON DIJON MUSTARD
1 TABLESPOON WORCESTERSHIRE SAUCE

TO SERVE
4 BURGER BUNS, OR 8 SMALL BUNS FOR SLIDERS (SEE PAGE 159 FOR HOMEMADE)
BEEF TOMATOES, THICKLY SLICED
ROUND LETTUCE, SEPARATED INTO INDIVIDUAL LEAVES AND STALKS TRIMMED
LARGE GHERKINS, THINLY SLICED
FRITES (SEE PAGE 180)

Mix the steak and pork mince together in a large bowl with your hands. Add all the remaining ingredients, ensuring that you sprinkle the salt in, and mix together until evenly incorporated.

Divide the mixture into four equal portions (or eight for sliders) and, preferably using an 85ml ring mould, shape into rounds. Place on a tray, cover with clingfilm and chill in the fridge until needed.

For the black pepper glaze, mix together the vinegar, sugar and soy sauce in a saucepan and cook until reduced by half.

Remove from the heat and mix in the Marmite, then leave to cool. The glaze should then coat the back of the spoon, so if it's too thin, return the pan to the heat and reduce further.

For the cheese slice, heat 200ml of the milk with the cheese in a saucepan until the cheese has melted completely. Add the flour and breadcrumbs, beat in and cook over a gentle heat, stirring frequently, for about 10 minutes until the floury taste has been cooked out. Whisk in the remaining 75ml milk.

Transfer the cheese mixture to a blender and whizz until really smooth. Season with salt. Add the whole egg, egg yolk, mustard and Worcestershire sauce and whizz again until well incorporated.

Line a tray with clingfilm and pour the mixture into the tray. Leave to set at room temperature.

Preheat the oven to 200°C/gas mark 6. Heat a cast-iron (ovenproof) frying pan until smoking hot. Add the burgers and sear on one side for 2 minutes, then flip over and cook for 30 seconds. Transfer the pan to the oven and cook for 4 minutes.

Remove from the oven, brush the tops of the burgers with the black pepper glaze and place a slice of the cheese mixture on top. Return to the oven for 1 minute.

Remove from the oven and gently brown the cheese with a blowtorch or place under a medium grill for 1–2 minutes. Leave to rest.

Split and toast the burger buns, then brush the inside of the buns with the black pepper glaze.

To serve, place a lettuce leaf on each bun bottom, followed by a slice of tomato, then the burger. Lay three slices of gherkin over each burger and prop the lid of the bun against the rest of the burger. Serve with some frites (see page 180) on the side.

OX CHEEK COBBLER

Cobblers, cobbles. It means a stoned pathway – or part of the male anatomy! You'll be pleased to know that this is neither. It is a delicious, slow cooked dish with a wonderful dumpling-type scone on top. I use ox cheeks with this because they are fantastically gooey, rich and moreish, and very easy to cook. So check out my cobblers!

1 TABLESPOON VEGETABLE OIL
2 WHOLE OX CHEEKS, SKINNED AND
   EACH SLICED INTO 6 PIECES
1 LARGE CARROT, PEELED AND CUT
   INTO 2.5CM DICE
2 ONIONS, CUT INTO 2.5CM DICE
1 LEEK, WASHED AND CUT INTO 2.5CM DICE
3 CELERY STICKS, PEELED AND CUT
   INTO 2.5CM DICE
½ HARD CELERIAC OR SWEDE, PEELED AND
   CUT INTO 2.5CM DICE
3 GARLIC CLOVES, ROUGHLY CHOPPED
100G PLAIN FLOUR
KNOB OF BUTTER
2 BAY LEAVES
3 SPRIGS OF THYME
3 SPRIGS OF TARRAGON
6 BLACK PEPPERCORNS
500ML GOOD-QUALITY RED WINE
500ML HOT BEEF STOCK

FOR THE COBBLER TOPPING
230G PLAIN FLOUR
30G SALTED BUTTER, CHILLED AND GRATED
100G BLUE CHEESE, CRUMBLED
1 TABLESPOON CHOPPED TARRAGON
1 TABLESPOON CHOPPED CHERVIL
1 TABLESPOON CHOPPED PARSLEY
1 TEASPOON MUSTARD POWDER
2 MEDIUM EGGS, BEATEN
3 TABLESPOONS MILK
PINCH OF SALT
110G BUTTER, MELTED

Preheat the oven to 180°C/gas mark 4.

Heat the oil in a flameproof casserole dish, add the ox cheek pieces and cook until browned and sealed on all sides.

Add the carrot, onions, leek, celery, celeriac or swede, and garlic to the dish and stir to mix.

Add the flour and butter then the herbs and peppercorns. Pour in the red wine and cook gently, stirring, for 5 minutes.

Stir in the beef stock, then put the lid on the dish and place in the oven for 1 hour 40 minutes until the beef is tender. Remove from the oven.

Prepare the cobbler topping while the beef is cooking. Mix together the flour, butter, cheese, herbs and mustard powder in a bowl.

Add the beaten eggs and milk and mix until the mixture comes together into a dough. Season with the salt.

Divide the mixture into 8–10 pieces, depending on how big you want your cobbles.

Remove the dish from the oven, lift off the lid and place the balls on top of the beef. Bake, uncovered, for a further 25 minutes.

Remove the dish from the oven and brush the cobbles with the melted butter to glaze. Serve with some buttered seasonal cabbage.

SERVES 4–6

BEEF RENDANG

Dave, my loyal old sous chef, loved Malaysian and Thai flavours and cooked this little baby a number of times for me and the gang. Although it's a simple dish, it has great flavour and complexity on the palate. You can use pork if you prefer, or even lamb, but beef is the best.

SERVES 4–6

1 TEASPOON CUMIN SEEDS
1 TABLESPOON CORIANDER SEEDS
2 CLOVES
2 SHALLOTS, ROUGHLY CHOPPED
3 GARLIC CLOVES, ROUGHLY CHOPPED
2 RED CHILLIES, DESEEDED OR NOT – IT'S UP TO YOU! – AND ROUGHLY CHOPPED
70G FRESH GINGER, PEELED AND GRATED
SPLASH OF SUNFLOWER OIL
500G BRAISING BEEF, DICED (OX CHEEK IS BEST)
400ML CAN COCONUT MILK
4 CARDAMOM PODS, CRACKED
4 KAFFIR LIME LEAVES
1 CINNAMON STICK
1 LEMONGRASS STALK
4 CORIANDER ROOTS (OPTIONAL)

TO GARNISH

1 RED CHILLI, THINLY SLICED
2 SPRING ONIONS, THINLY SLICED
50G CRISPY FRIED SHALLOTS (AVAILABLE READY-PREPARED FROM CHINESE SUPERMARKETS)
6 SPRIGS OF CORIANDER

Put the cumin and coriander seeds and cloves in a dry frying pan and gently heat until lightly toasted and aromatic.

Tip the toasted spices into a mortar and grind with a pestle to a fine powder.

Put the shallots, garlic, chillies, ginger and ground spices into a blender and whizz to a paste. Set aside.

Heat the oil in a medium saucepan or cast-iron braising pan, add the beef and cook until browned and sealed on all sides. Remove from the pan and set aside.

Add the spice paste to the pan and sweat over a gentle heat for 5 minutes.

Return the beef to the pan and stir in the coconut milk along with the remaining ingredients.

Add cold water to cover, bring to a very gentle simmer and leave to braise gently for 3 hours, topping up with water as necessary, until the beef is very soft and tender.

Once the beef is cooked, cook gently until the liquid has reduced to a thick sauce.

Serve the beef in a large sharing bowl, scattered with the thinly sliced chilli and spring onions, crispy fried shallots and sprigs of coriander, along with steamed jasmine rice.

USING A PIECE OF BEEF SUITABLE TO SLOW COOKING REALLY MAKES THI DISH AND IT'S KINDE TO YOUR POCKET TOO.

a moment
on the lips

It was sunny afternoon, my big sister Gaynor and I were on our first big solo outing – a trip to the local shops for Mom. I was 9ish, maybe younger, and I was so excited to be let loose. Gaynor was given the list, and the bag, and a couple of notes, as in £1 notes – it was that long ago.

Off we went, holding hands and skipping, yep skipping. We got to the shops and did what we had to do. Mom had also given us money for a pot of tea and cream cake, so when we were finished, we headed to a café called Jack Orners, where I had a massive chocolate eclair. I was in heaven. We finished up and skipped back home. We were still very excited and full of beans, so we played in the garden. One giant boot and the ball went over the hedge and hit next door's greenhouse – BOOM! 'Get in!' Mom shouted.

I ran towards the door. As I got close, Mom tried to give me a clip round the ear, but I ducked and swerved and head-butted the doorframe. I continued to run, holding my head. I was shocked and bleeding and dizzy, and when I got to the end of the hall I passed out, wet myself and woke up in hospital.

Mom was so upset, but it was my own fault. I never really played football in the garden after that, and I didn't have a cream cake for a while either.

WHITE + DARK CHOCOLATE CHEESECAKE WITH BANANA 'NON'-ICE CREAM

Count on your hands how many people don't love cheese-cake – easy, not many! Now count on your hands how many people love cheesecake – everyone! That's how many! Now, I'm telling you, chocolate cheesecake is another level. It's cheesecake and chocolate; what more can I say? What's great is that the chocolate gives it a velvety texture, plus it helps it to set, so you get to eat it sooner. Now that's a bonus!

150G DIGESTIVE BISCUITS, CRUSHED
½ TEASPOON GROUND CINNAMON
½ TEASPOON GROUND GINGER
80G SALTED BUTTER
400G SOFT CREAM CHEESE
50ML DOUBLE CREAM
1 VANILLA POD, SPLIT LENGTHWAYS AND
   SEEDS SCRAPED OUT
150G WHITE CHOCOLATE, MELTED
1 TABLESPOON BRANDY (OR OTHER BROWN
   SPIRIT, SUCH AS DARK RUM)
150G DARK CHOCOLATE, MELTED

FOR THE BANANA 'NON'-ICE CREAM
3 RIPE BANANAS
SPLASH OF BANANA LIQUEUR
1 TABLESPOON BROWN SUGAR
300ML WHIPPING CREAM, WHIPPED
   TO SOFT PEAKS

Mix together the biscuits, cinnamon and ginger in a mixing bowl.

Melt the butter in a saucepan, then pour over the crushed biscuit mixture and mix together well.

Line the base of a 20–22cm flan tin with the biscuit mixture, pressing it down firmly using the back of a spoon, cover and chill in the fridge for 2–4 hours hours until firm.

Divide the cream cheese between two separate bowls.

Add the cream and vanilla seeds to one of the bowls and mix together, then fold the melted white chocolate into the cream cheese and vanilla mixture.

Add the brandy to the melted dark chocolate, then fold it into the other bowl.

Spoon the chocolate mixtures, alternating one at a time, onto the biscuit base, then take a spoon and swirl the mixture to create a marbled effect. Leave to set in the fridge for 2 hours.

For the banana 'non'-ice cream, put the bananas in a blender and whizz to a smooth purée. Mix in the banana liqueur and sugar, then fold in the whipped cream.

Transfer the mixture to a lidded freezer-proof container and place in the freezer for about 6 hours until set. Stir occasionally while freezing.

Once both have set, cut the cheesecake into nice big slices and serve with a generous scoop of the banana 'non'-ice cream.

SERVES 6

WHITE + DARK CHOCOLATE
CHEESECAKE WITH BANANA
'NON'-ICE CREAM

PINEAPPLE SKEWERS

Pineapple is a particular favourite of mine. As a child, I only ever had it out of a tin, and I thought it was great, but freshly carved, it is a wonder to behold – so long as it's ripe. Using the vanilla pods as the skewers is so clever, but sadly I can't take the credit. It's been done for years. Nevertheless, I still love it, and it makes me smile. And as you know, I love food, especially if it makes me smile, that's my job! These skewers are sweet, aromatic and very delicious. Now that will make you smile!

MAKES 4

500ML PINEAPPLE JUICE
2 TABLESPOONS BROWN SUGAR
5 VANILLA PODS, 1 SPLIT LENGTHWAYS,
    SEEDS SCRAPED OUT AND RESERVED
½ CINNAMON STICK
1 BAY LEAF
1 STAR ANISE
1 LARGE PINEAPPLE, SKIN, EYES AND CORE
    REMOVED, THEN CUT IN HALF
600ML WHIPPING CREAM
50G ICING SUGAR
KNOB OF BUTTER
25G CASTER SUGAR
SMALL SPLASH OF RUM

Put the pineapple juice, brown sugar, the split, scraped-out vanilla pod, cinnamon stick, bay leaf and star anise in a wide saucepan and bring to a simmer.

Add the pineapple to the liquid and simmer for 20 minutes until tender.

Remove the pineapple from the poaching liquid and leave to cool.

Strain the poaching liquid through a sieve back into the pan, then cook until reduced to a thick glaze.

Cut the pineapple into 2.5cm-thick pieces and thread onto the remaining four vanilla pods.

Whip the cream and icing sugar with the reserved vanilla seeds to soft peaks and set aside.

Heat a frying pan, add the butter and melt, then add the pineapple skewers and roast over a medium-high heat, turning frequently, until beginning to colour evenly. Sprinkle in the caster sugar and continue to roast until golden brown. Add the rum and carefully ignite to flambé.

Transfer the pineapple to individual plates and cover with the glaze. Serve with the whipped vanilla cream.

CREME BRULEE

Crème brûlée comes in many forms. I serve it in an egg shell, but you already know that! This is a classic. God, I must have said classic 1,000,000 times. Like the way I used zeros instead of words? It's looks better and I am getting paid by the letter. Shit, do numbers count? Anyway, this is cooked the French way in a bain-marie. This is the way I was taught on the pastry section when I worked in Lyon. The 'proper' way, the French would say, and though I cook it on a stove it has a warm, professional feel in a bain-marie. A gentle, long and slow method, and very grown-up. Serve with Pistachio and Hazelnut Biscotti (see page 128).

500ML DOUBLE CREAM
2 VANILLA PODS, SPLIT LENGTHWAYS
  AND SEEDS SCRAPED OUT
6 LARGE EGG YOLKS
50G CASTER SUGAR

Preheat the oven to 160°C/gas mark 3.

Line a deep roasting tin with a clean cloth and place four 175ml ramekins on top. Lining it prevents direct heat from the tray. Set aside until needed.

Put the cream in a saucepan with the vanilla pods and seeds and bring to the boil, then simmer and reduce for 2 minutes.

In the bowl of a stand mixer fitted with the whisk attachment (or use a mixing bowl and an electric hand whisk), whisk together the egg yolks and sugar until thick, pale and fluffy. Pour over the hot cream and whisk until fully incorporated. Pass through a fine sieve into a jug and leave to rest for 5 minutes.

Skim the froth off the top of the mixture with a ladle, stir the mixture gently with a spoon, then pour evenly into the ramekins.

Pour boiling water into the roasting tin to come one-third of the way up the sides of the ramekins. Bake for 17–20 minutes, turning the tray halfway through to ensure even cooking – a crème brûlée should have a slight wobble in the middle.

Remove from the oven and put the ramekins on a wire rack to cool, then refrigerate until ready to serve.

SERVES 4

CHRISTMAS EASY-BAKED ALASKA

It's the most wonderful time of the year, as the song goes. And yes, it is, but it can sometimes get a bit boring (the food, I mean). It's great to have classic Christmas cheer, apart from sprouts. They're awful. I hate sprouts. They smell and taste as bad (little tip – cover them with bacon and chestnuts). No!, that's what I say to sprouts. This Christmas pud, on the other hand, is a big YES! It's fun, it has ice cream in it, and it tastes like Christmas, in a good way! Oh, and it doesn't make you fart!

½ BUNCH OF BASIL
250G CHRISTMAS BRANDY MINCEMEAT
1 LITRE DOUBLE CREAM VANILLA ICE CREAM
200ML STOCK SYRUP (SEE PAGE 143)
190ML DARK RUM
30 X 15CM VANILLA SPONGE (SEE PAGE 141), COOLED
4 EGG WHITES
400G CASTER SUGAR

Chop the basil and mix into the mincemeat in a bowl.

In the bowl of a stand mixer fitted with the paddle attachment, beat the ice cream until softened, but be careful not to overbeat it, as it will melt.

Add the mincemeat to the ice cream and mix together.

Lay out three pieces of clingfilm on a work surface side by side so that they overlap each other by half. Spoon the ice-cream mixture into the middle and use the clingfilm to roll it into a 7.5cm-thick cylinder. Place in the freezer for 24 hours.

Warm the stock syrup and 40ml of the dark rum in a saucepan, then pour over the sponge to soak it.

In the bowl of the stand mixer fitted with the whisk attachment, whisk the egg whites until soft peaks form then, whisking constantly, add the sugar, 1 tablespoon at a time, whisking until stiff and glossy.

Remove the clingfilm from the ice cream, then lay the ice cream on the sponge and, using a large palette knife, carefully cover with the meringue mixture.

Use a blowtorch to lightly brown the meringue.

Warm the remaining rum in a saucepan, carefully ignite and pour over the Alaska. Serve!!!

SERVES 6

PASSION FRUIT PARFAIT WITH CRISPY MERINGUE

I scream, you scream, we all love ice cream. Well, 99.9 per cent of people do and I'm in that gang. Parfait is like ice cream but has more of a solid texture. With the passion fruit it has a cheeky sour kick, which is delicious and also great with chocolate, so that's another excuse to make it.

MAKES 4

FOR THE PARFAIT
100ML DOUBLE CREAM
125ML PASSION FRUIT JUICE

FOR THE ITALIAN MERINGUE
1 EGG WHITE
60G CASTER SUGAR

FOR THE CRISPY MERINGUE
2 EGG WHITES
175G CASTER SUGAR
PINCH OF SALT
½ TEASPOON WHITE WINE VINEGAR

FOR THE SYRUP
100G CASTER SUGAR
100ML PASSION FRUIT JUICE

First make the parfait. Whip the cream in a bowl until soft peaks form, then add the passion fruit juice and whip until smooth – don't overwhip, as this will cause the cream to split.

To make the Italian meringue, put the egg white in a mixing bowl and line a baking tray with silicone paper.

Put the sugar in a small saucepan, just cover with cold water and set over a medium–high heat. When the temperature reaches 110°C (use a sugar thermometer), start whisking the egg white with an electric hand whisk on a low speed. Once the temperature of the sugar syrup reaches 120°C (hard-ball stage), the egg white should have tripled in volume. Increase the whisk speed to high and pour in the sugar syrup, then continue to whisk on high speed until the meringue has cooled.

Fold the parfait mixture into the meringue with a whisk, ensuring that it is thoroughly mixed, then spoon onto the lined tray and place in the freezer for a minimum of 6 hours, preferably overnight.

For the crispy meringue: Preheat the oven to 100°C/gas mark ¼. Line a baking tray with silicone paper.

In the bowl of a stand mixer (or use a mixing bowl and an electric hand whisk), whisk the egg whites until soft peaks form then, whisking constantly, add the sugar, 1 tablespoon at a time, along with the salt and vinegar, whisking until stiff and glossy. Spread the mixture thinly onto the silicone paper and bake for 15 minutes, then reduce the oven temperature to 90°C and bake for a further 45 minutes, or until crisp.

Remove from the oven and use a cutter to cut the meringue into the desired shapes, then leave to cool on a wire rack.

For the syrup: mix together the sugar and passion fruit juice in a saucepan and heat until the temperature of the syrup reaches 108°C (use a sugar thermometer). Remove the pan from the heat, leave to cool, then chill in the fridge for 2 hours before serving.

To serve: Using a small knife, carefully cut around the edge of each ring mould to release the parfait, then turn out onto a plate. Scatter over the meringue and decorate with flicks of the passion fruit syrup.

PROFITEROLES +ECLAIRS

They're French, so French you will feel French when you eat them, well sort of. Ask for them anywhere and they will know what you want. They are the superstar, the megastar, the global star of the dessert world. A red carpet walker, an Oscar winner for lifetime achievement. Hats off to the eighth wonder of the world – The Chocolate Eclair!

The classic approach is to fill the profiteroles and eclairs with Chantilly cream and dip them in chocolate fondant, but feel free to create your own unique combinations, such as filling them with the chocolate and covering with the salted caramel – the choice is yours!

MAKES 24
PROFITEROLES
OR 8 ECLAIRS

FOR THE CHOUX PASTRY
50G SALTED BUTTER
½ TEASPOON SALT
75G PLAIN FLOUR
½ TEASPOON CASTER SUGAR
2 LARGE EGGS

FOR THE CHANTILLY CREAM
200ML WHIPPING CREAM
60G CASTER SUGAR
1 VANILLA POD, SPLIT LENGTHWAYS AND
    SEEDS SCRAPED OUT
½ TEASPOON VANILLA EXTRACT

FOR THE CRÈME PÂTISSIÈRE
750ML FULL-FAT MILK
2 VANILLA PODS, SPLIT LENGTHWAYS AND
    SEEDS SCRAPED OUT
180G LARGE EGG YOLKS (ABOUT 9)
140G CASTER SUGAR
80G PLAIN FLOUR, SIFTED

Preheat the oven to 190°C/gas mark 5. Line two baking trays with silicone paper.

For the choux pastry: Put 125ml water, the butter and salt in a heavy-based saucepan and bring to the boil.

Sift together the flour and sugar, add to the pan all in one go and stir well with a wooden spoon to ensure that no lumps form. Cook over a medium heat, stirring, for 4–5 minutes until the mixture comes away from the sides of the pan and forms a smooth ball. Remove from the heat and continue to beat the dough for 1 minute to dry it out. Then beat in the eggs, one at a time, mixing well between each addition, until the mixture is smooth.

Transfer the choux dough to a piping bag fitted with a plain 1cm piping nozzle. For profiteroles, pipe domes about 3cm in diameter and 3cm in height onto the prepared baking trays, spacing them 8cm apart, as they will puff outwards. For éclairs, pipe lines about 12.5cm in length and 3cm in width.

Bake for 15–20 minutes until golden brown and firm to the touch, then reduce the oven temperature to 160°C/gas mark 3 and bake for a

further 5 minutes to dry out. Remove from the oven and leave to cool for 1 minute, then prick a small hole in the base of each choux ball or eclair to release the steam and prevent them from turning soggy. Transfer to a wire rack and leave to cool completely.

When ready to assemble, pipe your chosen filling into the holes for profiteroles or slice lengthways and pipe inside for éclairs.

For the Chantilly cream: Put the cream, sugar, vanilla seeds and vanilla extract in a mixing bowl and whip until thick. Spoon the mixture into a piping bag fitted with a 3mm piping nozzle and refrigerate until required.

For the crème pâtissière: Put the milk, vanilla pods and seeds in a heavy-based saucepan and bring to the boil over a medium heat. Remove from the heat, cover with clingfilm and leave to infuse for 20 minutes, then remove the vanilla pods.

In the bowl of a stand mixer fitted with the whisk attachment (or use a mixing bowl and an electric hand whisk), whisk together the egg yolks and sugar until thick, pale and fluffy. Add the sifted flour and whisk until smooth.

Pour half the infused milk onto the egg yolk mixture and whisk until no lumps remain. Pass the mixture through a fine sieve into the remaining infused milk in the pan, then whisk constantly over a medium heat until it comes to the boil. Reduce the heat and simmer, stirring with a spatula, for 4–5 minutes.

Remove the pan from the heat and pour the crème pâtissière into a shallow dish or tray. Cover the surface with clingfilm to prevent a skin forming and place in the fridge to cool.

FOR THE FONDANT GLAZE
100G DARK CHOCOLATE (70 PER CENT
  COCOA SOLIDS), CHOPPED
300G ICING SUGAR
1 TABLESPOON GLUCOSE

FOR THE SALTED CARAMEL
100ML DOUBLE CREAM
1 VANILLA POD, SPLIT LENGTHWAYS AND
  SEEDS SCRAPED OUT
200G GRANULATED SUGAR
30G GLUCOSE
150G SALTED BUTTER, SOFTENED AND DICED
3G MALDON SEA SALT, OR TO TASTE

For the glaze: Put the chocolate in a bowl. Combine the icing sugar and glucose with 65ml water in a pan and warm over a low heat, stirring constantly, until the temperature reaches 33°C (use a sugar thermometer). Remove from the heat, pour the contents over the chocolate and stir gently until all the chocolate has melted.

Dip the filled profiteroles or eclairs into the chocolate glaze to coat the tops. Alternatively, stack the profiteroles on a serving plate and pour the glaze over the top.

For the caramel: Put the cream, vanilla pod and seeds in a heavy-based saucepan and bring to the boil over a medium heat. Remove from the heat, cover with clingfilm and leave to infuse for 20 minutes, then remove the vanilla pods.

Heat 100g of the sugar with the glucose in a separate heavy-based saucepan over a medium heat until it starts to melt, then stir gently with a heatproof spatula until a light caramel forms and the sugar crystals have all dissolved. Add the remaining sugar and continue to cook until you have an amber caramel.

Reduce the heat to low, carefully add the cream mixture and whisk slowly until fully incorporated. Remove the pan from the heat and leave to cool for 1 minute.

Add the butter, cube by cube, whisking until fully emulsified with the caramel. Add the salt and mix well, then taste the caramel – bearing in mind it will be hot! – and add more salt if desired.

Pour into a shallow tray and leave to cool. Keep at room temperature if using the same day, otherwise store in an airtight container in the fridge for up to two weeks.

POACHED SUMMER FRUITS IN BASIL + CARDAMOM WITH SABAYON + WHITE CHOCOLATE

Sabayon can be served hot, tepid or cool. If you want to serve it warm, make it at the last minute. If you want to glaze the sabayon with a blowtorch (or place it under the grill) you will need to make it ahead of time.

SERVES 4

FOR THE POACHED FRUITS
300G CASTER SUGAR
4 CARDAMOM PODS, CRUSHED
8 LARGE BASIL LEAVES, ROUGHLY CHOPPED
ZEST AND JUICE OF 1 LEMON
3 PEACHES, HALVED AND STONED
3 APRICOTS, HALVED AND STONED
15 FRESH STRAWBERRIES, HULLED BUT
    KEPT WHOLE

FOR THE SABAYON
6 EGG YOLKS
2 TABLESPOONS SHERRY OR MADEIRA
70G CASTER SUGAR, PLUS EXTRA IF
    REQUIRED TO TASTE
SQUEEZE OF LEMON JUICE, OR TO TASTE
100G WHITE CHOCOLATE, PLACED IN
    THE FREEZER FOR 2 HOURS UNTIL
    HALF FROZEN

For the poached fruits, put the sugar, cardamom pods and 600ml water in a saucepan and bring to a simmer, stirring until the sugar has dissolved.

Add the basil and lemon zest and juice, and leave to infuse over a low heat for 20 minutes.

Cook the peaches and apricots, in batches, in the poaching syrup for 3–5 minutes until just tender. Remove with a slotted spoon and set aside.

Cook the strawberries in the syrup for just 1 minute, then remove with a slotted spoon and set aside. Reserve the poaching syrup.

Leave the fruit to cool slightly, then return it to the poaching syrup, cover with clingfilm and leave to cool completely in the fridge.

For the sabayon: Whisk together the egg yolks, sherry or Madeira and sugar in a stainless steel bowl. Set the bowl over a pan of hot water and whisk constantly for 4–5 minutes until the mixture has the consistency of lightly whipped cream and the sauce is cooked – clear the base of the bowl constantly with the whisk to prevent the eggs from scrambling and don't allow it to become so hot that it can't be touched with a finger.

Taste the sabayon and add more sugar and a squeeze of lemon to taste.

Once the sabayon is thick, foamy and tripled in volume, remove the bowl from the pan.

Drain the fruit from the poaching syrup (you can keep this in the fridge for 5–10 days to reuse), pat dry with kitchen paper and scatter over plates or bowls using your own artistic flair. Spoon four or five dollops of sabayon over the fruits, then use a blowtorch to brown the sabayon, or place under the grill. Grate the white chocolate over the top and serve immediately.

FAST FRUIT FRUMBLE

Let's get ready to rumble! No, it's not a fight, it's a crumble. Yes, a crumble. Not really party fare, but packed with flavour. It's great for capturing the seasons as you change the fruit. Me, I like more crumble than fruit, so that may be where the fight starts - over the topping that is!

MAKES 4

400G PLAIN FLOUR
150G CASTER SUGAR
200G SALTED BUTTER, CHILLED AND DICED, PLUS 70G
100G SKINNED HAZELNUTS, CHOPPED
2 LARGE APPLES, PEELED, CORED AND CHOPPED
2 PEARS, PEELED CORED AND CHOPPED
100G BROWN SUGAR
100ML RUBY PORT
ZEST OF 1 ORANGE
1 TABLESPOON GROUND CINNAMON
200G FRESH BLACKBERRIES, CRUSHED
200G FRESH RASPBERRIES, CRUSHED
ICING SUGAR, FOR DUSTING

Preheat the oven to 180°C/gas mark 4.

Mix together the flour and caster sugar in a mixing bowl. Add the 200g butter and rub in with your fingertips until the mixture has a crumb consistency.

Stir in the hazelnuts.

Spread the crumble mixture onto a baking tray and bake for 8–10 minutes until golden brown.

Meanwhile, melt the remaining 70g butter in a large saucepan, add the apples and pears and cook until the fruit begins to soften.

Add the brown sugar, port, orange zest and cinnamon to the pan and cook for 5 minutes.

Remove the pan from the heat and stir in the blackberries and raspberries.

Pour the fruit mixture into an ovenproof serving dish, sprinkle over the crumble, then bake for 10 minutes.

Remove the dish from the oven and dust with icing sugar. Serve with cream or custard.

PISTACHIO + HAZELNUT BISCOTTI

MAKES 50–60 PIECES

40G SALTED BUTTER
ZEST AND JUICE OF 1 LEMON
3 EGGS
2 EGG YOLKS
275G CASTER SUGAR
425G PLAIN FLOUR
1 TEASPOON BAKING POWDER
125G SKINNED HAZELNUTS, TOASTED
125G SKINNED (GREEN) PISTACHIO NUTS

Preheat the oven to 160°C/gas mark 3. Line a baking tray with silicone paper.

In the bowl of a stand mixer fitted with the whisk attachment, whisk the butter with the lemon zest and juice. Add the whole eggs, egg yolks and sugar and whisk until thick, pale and fluffy.

Sift together the flour and baking powder, add to the egg mixture and, using the paddle attachment, mix thoroughly. Fold through the nuts on a low speed, then leave to stand for 5 minutes to toughen the gluten.

Spread the mixture onto the lined baking tray, divide in half and shape into two long loaves. Bake for 20–25 minutes until beginning to turn golden brown. Remove from the oven and leave to cool slightly. Reduce the temperature to 150°C/gas mark 2.

Using a serrated knife, cut the loaves into slices ½cm thick and put on two large baking trays lined with silicone paper. Bake for another 6–7 minutes, being careful not to colour the biscotti any further.

Remove from the oven and leave the to cool on a wire rack.

FROZEN RHUBARB +CRANBERRY MERINGUE

This is clever and so refreshing. It's not a meringue, it's not a sorbet, it's both. No actually, it's a cloud! Believe it or not, it's great as a pre-dessert or as a big bowl of meringuey-deliciousness, if that's even a word?

FOR THE RHUBARB JUICE
25 LARGE RHUBARB STICKS (ABOUT 1KG)
TINY PINCH OF SALT
30G CASTER SUGAR
4 DROPS NATURAL RED FOOD COLOURING

FOR THE FROZEN MERINGUE
75G CASTER SUGAR
1 BRONZE GELATINE LEAF, SOAKED IN COLD
   WATER FOR 5 MINUTES
100ML CRANBERRY JUICE
18G ALBÚMINA POWDERED EGG WHITE
2 TABLESPOONS GRAND MARNIER

FOR THE POACHED RHUBARB AND CRANBERRIES
1 LITRE CRANBERRY JUICE
200G CASTER SUGAR
1 VANILLA POD, SPLIT LENGTHWAYS
8 X 40CM RHUBARB STICKS (130G), HALVED
100G FROZEN CRANBERRIES, DEFROSTED
   (CHEAPER AND EASY TO BUY, BUT FEEL
   FREE TO USE FRESH)
25G PISTACHIO NUTS, TOASTED AND
   CHOPPED, PER SERVING

For the rhubarb juice, process the rhubarb through a juicer, then skim off the froth and measure 250ml. Mix in the salt and sugar until dissolved, then mix in the food colouring. Set aside.

For the frozen meringue, line a tray about 30 x 25cm and 7cm deep with clingfilm and place in the freezer.

Heat 75ml water and the sugar gently in a small saucepan, stirring until the sugar has dissolved. Remove from the heat, add the drained, squeezed-out gelatine leaf and leave until melted, stirring occasionally.

In the bowl of a stand mixer fitted with the whisk attachment, whisk together the rhubarb juice, cranberry juice and albúmina on a low speed, then increase the speed to medium. When the mixture has tripled in volume, reduce the speed and slowly add the gelatine mixture. Whisk on a medium speed until the meringue has tripled in volume again, then add the Grand Marnier and whisk for a further 10 seconds.

Remove the lined tray from the freezer and, using a spatula, scrape the meringue gently into the tray. Smooth off the top or leave for a rustic, uneven effect. Place in the freezer for a minimum of 6 hours, preferably overnight.

For the poached rhubarb and cranberries, put 750ml of the cranberry juice, the sugar and vanilla pod in a large sauté pan and bring to a simmer over a medium heat. Add the rhubarb to the pan along with the remaining cranberry juice if the rhubarb is not completely covered. Simmer gently for 5–10 minutes, or until a knife penetrates the rhubarb with little resistance.

Remove the rhubarb and put on a tray to cool, then cook the poaching liquid until reduced by one-third and stir in the cranberries.

Remove the pan from the heat and leave to stand until the cranberries are softened, then chill in the fridge ready to serve.

To serve, place one piece of the poached rhubarb at room temperature in a large serving bowl and sprinkle with the pistachios. Spoon the cranberries and some of the chilled poaching liquid around the piece of rhubarb, then add a large scoop of the frozen meringue on top. Serve immediately.

Note
This is the minimum you can make for the quantities to be large enough for the meringue to be whisked and set. The frozen meringue will keep in the freezer for up to seven days.

SERVES 16–20

FROZEN RHUBARB
+ CRANBERRY MERINGUE

PARIS-BREST

This French classic pays homage to a famous bike ride – the shape represents a bicycle wheel. I first cooked it when I was fourteen. I found the recipe in a women's magazine at the dentist. When I told the teacher what I was cooking, she looked at me strangely and said, 'Choux pastry? You can't make choux pastry, you're fourteen years old!' 'Well,' I replied, 'if a woman can cook it out of a magazine, so can I!' I did cook it, and it turned out okay. Not exactly like the picture, but it was nice!

SERVES 6 OR
A FEW GREEDY
PEOPLE

FOR THE CHOUX PASTRY
100G SALTED BUTTER
PINCH OF SALT
200G STRONG WHITE BREAD FLOUR, SIFTED
4 LARGE EGGS
1 EGG YOLK, LIGHTLY BEATEN
FLAKED ALMONDS, FOR SPRINKLING

FOR THE PRALINE CREAM
SUNFLOWER OIL, FOR GREASING
150G CASTER SUGAR
150G SKINNED HAZELNUTS, TOASTED
PINCH OF SALT
300ML DOUBLE CREAM
1 VANILLA POD, SPLIT LENGTHWAYS, AND
    SEEDS SCRAPED OUT

TO SERVE
ICING SUGAR, FOR DUSTING
TOASTED CHOPPED HAZELNUTS OR PISTACHIO
    NUTS, FOR SPRINKLING

Preheat the oven to 180°C/gas mark 4. Using a pencil, draw a 20cm circle onto a sheet of silicone paper. Turn over and put on a baking tray.

Put 250ml cold water, the butter and salt in a heavy-based saucepan and bring to the boil. Add the flour, all in one go, and stir well with a wooden spoon to ensure that no lumps form. Cook over a medium heat, stirring, for 4–5 minutes until the mixture comes away from the sides of the pan and forms a smooth ball. Remove from the heat, leave to cool for 5 minutes, then beat in the whole eggs, one at a time, mixing well between each addition, until the mixture is smooth.

Transfer the mixture to a piping bag fitted with a plain 12mm piping nozzle. Pipe one ring, or 'crown', of choux dough, following the pencil line on the silicone paper, then pipe another ring inside the first, touching the inside. Finally, pipe a third ring of choux on top of, and overlapping, each of the first two rings.

Using a pastry brush, glaze the surface of the 'crown' with the egg yolk, then sprinkle the entire surface with flaked almonds. Bake for 15–20 minutes until the pastry has risen and is a nice golden colour. Remove from the oven and leave to cool.

For the praline cream, lay a sheet of lightly greased silicone paper on a baking tray.

Heat the sugar in a heavy-based saucepan over a medium heat until it starts to melt, then stir gently to evenly caramelise the sugar, until you have a golden brown caramel.

Pour the caramel over the prepared paper, being careful not to burn yourself. Sprinkle the hazelnuts evenly over the caramel, season with the salt and leave to cool completely.

Put half the cooled praline in a blender and whizz to a fine powder. Transfer to a clean, dry bowl. Add the remaining praline to the blender and pulse to achieve a coarser mix, then mix into the powdered praline.

Whip the cream with the vanilla seeds in a mixing bowl until soft peaks form. Add the praline to your own taste and sweetness, then whip to medium peaks and transfer to a piping bag fitted with a fluted nozzle.

Using a serrated knife, cut the crown in half horizontally. Pipe the praline cream onto the bottom half of the crown, forming large swirls. Replace the top half of the crown and refrigerate for 1 hour until set.

Remove from the fridge 30 minutes before serving, dust with icing sugar and sprinkle with chopped toasted hazelnuts or pistachios.

BLACKBERRY PARFAITS WITH POACHED PEARS +HONEYCOMB

Parfait, semi-frado, ice cream, they're all delicious! This is pretty easy to do. You can use other fruit according to the season, but this is blackberry, so push on!

SERVES 4

FOR THE PARFAITS
375G DOUBLE CREAM
500G BLACKBERRY PUREE
2 LARGE EGG WHITES
160G CASTER SUGAR

FOR THE POACHED PEARS
250G CASTER SUGAR
4 BAY LEAVES
1 VANILLA POD, SPLIT LENGTHWAYS
PINCH OF SALT
JUICE OF ½ LEMON
4 PEARS, PEELED

FOR THE HONEYCOMB
325G CASTER SUGAR
125G GLUCOSE
50G HONEY
15G BICARBONATE OF SODA

For the parfaits, whip the cream in a large bowl until soft peaks form, then fold in the blackberry purée. Line a baking tray with silicone paper.

Put the egg whites in the bowl of a stand mixer fitted with the whisk attachment (or use a mixing bowl and an electric hand whisk).

Put the sugar in a saucepan, just cover with cold water, and set over a medium–high heat. When the temperature of the sugar syrup reaches 110°C (use a sugar thermometer), start whisking the egg whites on a low speed. Once the temperature reaches 120°C (hard-ball stage), the whites should have tripled in volume. Increase the mixer speed to high, pour in the sugar syrup, then continue to whisk on a high speed until the meringue has cooled.

Fold half the blackberry cream mixture into the meringue, using a whisk to avoid lumps forming, then add the meringue mixture to the remaining blackberry cream mixture in the bowl, folding in with the whisk. Once thoroughly combined, spoon into the ring moulds and place in the freezer for 24 hours.

For the poached pears: Put 750ml cold water, the sugar, bay leaves, vanilla pod, salt and lemon juice in a pan large enough to accommodate the pears and bring to a simmer, stirring until the sugar has dissolved. Add the pears and

simmer for about 10 minutes, or until they are tender.Remove the pan from the heat and leave the pears to cool in the poaching liquid.

Lift the cooled pears out, set aside, and cook the poaching liquid until reduced by half. Reserve for glazing.

For the honeycomb: Line a baking tray with silicone paper.

Put the sugar, glucose, honey and 60ml water in a saucepan over a medium heat, stirring until the sugar has dissolved. Increase the heat and cook until the temperature of the syrup reaches 150°C (use a sugar thermometer), using a pastry brush dipped in water to wash the sides of the pan clean of any sugar crystals. Remove from the heat and very quickly whisk in the bicarbonate of soda. Pour the mixture onto the lined tray and leave to cool.

To serve: Remove the parfaits from the freezer and gently blowtorch the metal rings to release them.

Put a poached pear in the centre of a plate and place a parfait beside it. Drizzle with the poaching liquid.

Either snap off a large piece of honeycomb and grate it over the top or put a large piece in a plastic bag and gently beat with a rolling pin to produce bite-sized pieces, then scatter these over the parfait and pear.

MA'S BREAD + BUTTER PUDDING

My mom was a solid cook. No frills, just really good flavours. This is one of her best puddings, a real Sunday treat. Me, Gaz, Gem and Gaynor would eat up all our dinner, greens included, just so we'd be allowed pudding. It could be a cake, custard or baked riced pud or, the winner, bread and butter pudding! The best thing about it was that if any was left over we could have it cold the next day or later on for tea.

12 SLICES OF WHITE BREAD, CRUSTS ON
60G SALTED BUTTER, SOFTENED
60G DRIED FRUIT OF YOUR CHOICE
2 GENEROUS TABLESPOONS CLEAR HONEY
   OR GOLDEN SYRUP, FOR DRIZZLING
400ML FULL-FAT MILK
100ML DOUBLE CREAM
1 VANILLA POD, SPLIT LENGTHWAYS
30G CASTER SUGAR
1 TEASPOON QUATRE EPICES
ZEST OF 1 ORANGE
2 EGGS
15G BROWN SUGAR

SERVES 8

Preheat the oven to 180°C/gas mark 4.

Spread the bread slices with the butter and cut into triangles.

Layer the buttered bread triangles in an ovenproof dish, sprinkling in between with the dried fruit and drizzling with the honey or golden syrup.

Combine the milk, cream, vanilla pod, caster sugar, quatre épices and orange zest in a saucepan and warm through gently without boiling.

Whisk the eggs in a bowl, then slowly pour the warm milk mixture onto the eggs and whisk to combine.

Pour the egg mixture over the bread and then push down to ensure that the mixture sinks through to the base of the dish.

Sprinkle evenly with the brown sugar and then bake for 40–50 minutes until set and golden.

CHERRY CLAFOUTIS

If you're a purist you take out the cherry stones, but if you're hard core you leave them in. Me, I take them out, but only because I don't want to pay your dentist bill!

FOR THE CHERRIES
500G RIPE CHERRIES, STONED
75G CASTER SUGAR
75ML KIRSCH

FOR THE BATTER
40G SALTED BUTTER, DICED
6 LARGE EGG YOLKS
3 LARGE EGGS
150G CASTER SUGAR
½ TEASPOON VANILLA EXTRACT
375ML DOUBLE CREAM
75ML CHERRY BRANDY
300G STRONG WHITE BREAD FLOUR, SIFTED

FOR THE VANILLA ANGLAISE
375ML DOUBLE CREAM
375ML FULL-FAT MILK
2 VANILLA PODS, SPLIT LENGTHWAYS AND
    SEEDS SCRAPED OUT
9 LARGE EGG YOLKS
60G CASTER SUGAR
20ML DARK RUM

TO FINISH
BUTTER, FOR GREASING
CASTER SUGAR, FOR SPRINKLING
50G SALTED PISTACHIO NUTS, TOASTED
    AND CHOPPED
ICING SUGAR, FOR DUSTING

Mix the cherries, sugar and kirsh in a bowl, then leave to macerate at room temperature for 2 hours.

For the batter: Heat the butter in a small pan over a medium heat until it turns a nut brown (beurre noisette). Be careful not to colour it too much and burn it! Remove from the heat.

In the bowl of a stand mixer fitted with the whisk attachment (or use a mixing bowl and an electric hand whisk), whisk together the egg yolks, whole eggs, sugar and vanilla until thick and pale. Add the cream and cherry brandy and whisk together. Add 200g of the flour, one-third at a time, whisking after each addition until smooth.

Mix in the beurre noisette, then pass through a sieve into a bowl. Cover with clingfilm and chill for 24 hours.

Remove the batter from the fridge about 30 minutes before using to bring to room temperature and whisk in the remaining 100g flour until smooth.

For the vanilla anglaise: Put a large bowl half-filled with equal quantities of ice and water in the fridge.

Combine the cream, milk, vanilla pods and seeds in a saucepan and bring to the boil over a medium heat. Remove from the heat, leave to infuse for 30 minutes, then remove the vanilla pods.

In the bowl of a stand mixer fitted with the whisk attachment (or use a mixing bowl and an electric hand whisk), whisk together the egg yolks and sugar until thick, pale and fluffy.

Bring the cream mixture back up to just below boiling point and pour over the yolk mixture, whisking constantly. Pour into a clean pan, ensuring that you scrape all the mixture from the bowl with a spatula, and cook over a medium heat, stirring, until it reaches a temperature of 82°C (use a sugar thermometer).

Immediately pass the mixture through a fine sieve into a bowl. Put the bowl straight into iced water and stir the anglaise until cool, taking care not to splash the water into it. This stops the custard from overcooking and the eggs from scrambling.

Once cooled, whisk in the rum, pour into a jug, cover the surface with clingfilm and refrigerate until required.

To finish, preheat the oven to 180°C/gas mark 4. Grease a large round ovenproof dish with a little butter and evenly sprinkle with caster sugar, tapping out the excess.

Mix the macerated cherries and juice with the batter and pour into the prepared dish. Bake for 30–40 minutes until the top is slightly domed and golden, or a metal skewer inserted into the centre comes out clean.

Remove from the oven, sprinkle with the pistachios and dust with icing sugar. Serve immediately with a jug of the vanilla anglaise.

SERVES 6

SABLE BRETON WITH ALMOND ICE CREAM +ROASTED APRICOTS

Sablé. What a strange word. It means a biscuit. Crunchy but really buttery. It's really easy to make, plus you can freeze the mixture so you always have a solid pud on standby. It's particularly tasty served with cream and raspberries. Like a scone, but a bit a cooler. The only problem with it is that you can't really dunk it in your tea because it's so crumbly!

SERVES 4

FOR THE SABLE
400G CASTER SUGAR
8 EGG YOLKS
320G SALTED BUTTER, SOFTENED
2 VANILLA PODS, SPLIT LENGTHWAYS,
    AND SEEDS SCRAPED OUT
560G PLAIN FLOUR
24G BAKING POWDER

FOR THE APRICOTS
12 APRICOTS, HALVED AND STONED
50G CASTER SUGAR
15G PICKED ROSEMARY LEAVES
50G SALTED BUTTER
½ VANILLA POD, SPLIT LENGTHWAYS,
    AND SEEDS SCRAPED OUT

FOR THE ICE CREAM
400ML ALMOND MILK
300ML DOUBLE CREAM
100G FLAKED ALMONDS, TOASTED
4 MEDIUM EGG YOLKS
50G CASTER SUGAR
1 TEASPOON ALMOND EXTRACT

TO SERVE
TOASTED FLAKED ALMONDS

For the sable: In the bowl of a stand mixer fitted with the paddle attachment, beat together the sugar and egg yolks on a medium speed until pale. Beat in the butter and vanilla seeds, then add the flour and baking powder and beat until combined.

Roll out the dough on a tray to a thickness of 2cm. Cover with clingfilm and leave to rest in the fridge for a minimum of 2 hours before baking.

Preheat the oven to 180°C/gas mark 4.

Remove the dough from the fridge and either bake in one piece or, using a 4–5cm round cutter, cut into discs and place on baking trays. Bake for 16–20 minutes, or until golden brown with a brittle texture. Remove from the oven and leave to cool on a wire rack. Break into shards once cooled if baked in one piece.

For the apricots: Preheat the oven to 180°C/gas mark 4. Put the apricots, cut-side up, on a baking tray.

Put the sugar and rosemary in a blender and pulse until well blended, then sprinkle over the apricots.

Melt the butter in a small saucepan and add the vanilla seeds, then drizzle over the apricots. Roast for 6–7 minutes, or until tender.

For the ice cream: Mix together the almond milk, cream and 75g of the almonds in a saucepan and bring to the boil. Remove from the heat and leave to infuse for 30 minutes.

In the bowl of a stand mixer fitted with the whisk attachment (or use a mixing bowl and an electric hand whisk), whisk together the egg yolks, sugar and almond extract until thick, pale and fluffy.

Bring the milk and cream back up to just below boiling point and pour over the yolk mixture, whisking constantly. Pour into a clean pan, ensuring that you scrape all the mixture from the bowl with a spatula, and cook over a medium heat, stirring constantly, until it coats the back of a spoon. Remove from the heat, pass through a sieve into a bowl and leave to cool.

Churn in an ice-cream maker according to the manufacturer's instructions until frozen. Transfer to a lidded freezer-proof container and place in the freezer for a minimum of 4–5 hours, preferably overnight.

Place the sablé in the centre of each plate and add as many apricot halves as you fancy. Spoon the ice cream into the centre and sprinkle with almonds to finish.

GATEAU LIEGEOIS, GP STYLE

I've made this up. I have, really. It's inspired by a Belgian pudding (not French, as the name suggests), which dates back roughly to 1914. I've turned what was a dessert into a modern cake or gateau. It's a real showstopper, with a delicious coffee flavour and crunch from the tuile. If you want to blow people away, this is your man!

SERVES 6

FOR THE VANILLA SPONGE
150G SALTED BUTTER, SOFTENED
150G CASTER SUGAR
3 EGGS, BEATEN
½ TEASPOON VANILLA EXTRACT
150G SELF-RAISING FLOUR
1 TEASPOON BAKING POWDER

FOR THE COFFEE BUTTERCREAM
500G ICING SUGAR
250G SALTED BUTTER, SOFTENED
2 TEASPOONS INSTANT COFFEE GRANULES,
   DISSOLVED IN 2 TEASPOONS BOILING
   WATER

FOR THE CHOCOLATE TUILE
150G CASTER SUGAR
125G SALTED BUTTER, DICED
50G GLUCOSE
50ML FULL-FAT MILK
15G COCOA POWDER

TO FINISH
400ML DOUBLE CREAM
150G COCOA POWDER, FOR DUSTING

For the vanilla sponge, preheat the oven to 180°C/gas mark 4. Line two 23cm sandwich tins with silicone or greaseproof paper.

In the bowl of a stand mixer fitted with the paddle attachment (or use a mixing bowl and an electric hand mixer), beat together the butter and sugar until light and fluffy.

Add the eggs, one at a time, beating well after each addition. Add the vanilla extract and mix to combine.

Fold in the flour and baking powder and mix until combined.

Divide the mixture evenly between the prepared tins and bake for 18–20 minutes until golden and a metal skewer inserted into the centre comes out clean.

Remove the tins from the oven and leave the cakes to cool in the tins for 5 minutes before turning out onto a wire rack to cool completely.

For the coffee buttercream, using the stand mixer fitted with the paddle attachment (or hand mixer), beat together the icing sugar and butter until light and fluffy.

Add the coffee and continue beating until the mixture is light and smooth.

For the chocolate tuile, line a baking tray with silicone or greaseproof paper.

Put the sugar, butter, glucose and milk in a saucepan and bring to the boil, then add the cocoa powder and whisk thoroughly.

Remove the pan from the heat, spread the mixture onto the lined baking tray and bake for 10 minutes

Remove the tray from the oven and leave the tuile to cool and harden on the tray.

Once completely cool, break the tuile into shards.

To finish, spread the top of one of the sponges with the coffee buttercream, then place the second sponge on top.

Whip the double cream until soft peaks form, then use to cover the cake completely. Dust all over with the cocoa powder and decorate with the shards of chocolate tuile.

WHITE CHOCOLATE +RASPBERRY TRIFLE

If you have soaked sponge, fresh fruit, custard and jelly sitting on top of each other you have . . . a trifle. If those layers are amaretto soaked sponge, fresh raspberries, white chocolate custard, raspberry and rosewater jelly and the cheeky addition of crispy vanilla meringue, you may just have the best damn trifle in the world. This one was created by my right-hand man, Luke Butcher.

SERVES 4–6

FOR THE GENOISE SPONGE
60G SALTED BUTTER, DICED
120G CASTER SUGAR
4 LARGE EGGS
120G PLAIN FLOUR, SIFTED

FOR THE AMARETTO SYRUP
100G CASTER SUGAR
75ML AMARETTO LIQUEUR

FOR THE RASPBERRY PUREE
400G FRESH RASPBERRIES
125ML STOCK SYRUP (SEE OPPOSITE)
JUICE OF 1 LEMON
1 VANILLA POD, SPLIT LENGTHWAYS AND
   SEEDS SCRAPED OUT

FOR THE CUSTARD
300G WHITE CHOCOLATE
375ML FULL-FAT MILK
125ML DOUBLE CREAM
120ML EGG YOLKS (ABOUT 6)
50G CASTER SUGAR

FOR THE JELLY
700G FRESH RASPBERRIES
500G CASTER SUGAR
15 BRONZE GELATINE LEAVES
1 TEASPOON ROSEWATER, OR TO TASTE

FOR THE MERINGUE
265G CASTER SUGAR
1 TEASPOON CORNFLOUR
150ML EGG WHITES (ABOUT 5 LARGE)
1 TEASPOON RASPBERRY VINEGAR
1 TEASPOON VANILLA EXTRACT
30G FREEZE-DRIED RASPBERRY PIECES

TO ASSEMBLE
600G FRESH RASPBERRIES

For the sponge: Preheat the oven to 170°C/gas mark 3½. Grease a 30 x 25cm, 7cm deep, cake tin with butter and line it with silicone paper.

Heat the butter in a small pan over a medium heat until it turns nut brown (beurre noisette). Be careful not to colour the butter too much and burn it! Remove from the heat.

In the bowl of a stand mixer fitted with the whisk attachment (or use a mixing bowl and an electric hand whisk), whisk together the sugar and eggs until pale, thick and fluffy.

Gently fold the flour into the egg mixture, one-third at a time, being careful to avoid knocking too much air out of the mixture. Add the beurre noisette and fold in gently.

Pour the mixture into the prepared tin and bake in the centre of the oven for 25–30 minutes, or until a metal skewer inserted into the centre comes out clean. Remove from the oven and leave to cool in the tin for 15 minutes, then remove carefully and put on a wire rack to cool completely.

For the syrup: Bring 150ml cold water and the sugar to the boil in a saucepan, stirring until the sugar has dissolved.

Remove from the heat and whisk in the amaretto. Set aside at room temperature until required.

For the purée: Put all the ingredients in a saucepan set over a low–medium heat and simmer for 5 minutes. Remove from the heat, cover with a lid and leave to infuse for 10 minutes.

Remove the vanilla pod, pour the mixture into a blender and whizz for 3 minutes. Pass through a fine sieve into a bowl, cover with clingfilm and refrigerate until required.

For the custard: Place a large bowl half-filled with equal quantities of ice and water in the fridge.

Break the chocolate into pieces and melt in a heatproof bowl over a saucepan of barely simmering water.

Combine the milk and cream in a saucepan and bring to the boil over a medium heat, then remove from the heat.

In the bowl of a stand mixer fitted with the whisk attachment (or use a mixing bowl and an electric hand whisk), whisk together the egg yolks and sugar until thick, pale and fluffy.

Bring the milk mixture back up to just below boiling point and pour over the yolk mixture, whisking constantly. Pour into a clean saucepan, ensuring that you scrape all the mixture from the bowl with a spatula, and cook over a medium heat, stirring, until it reaches a temperature of 82°C (use a sugar thermometer).

Immediately pass the mixture through a fine sieve into a bowl. Put the bowl straight into iced water and stir the custard for 2 minutes until slightly cooled, taking care not to splash water into it. This process stops the custard from overcooking and the eggs from scrambling.

Measure 400ml of the custard into a jug, then pour this steadily into the melted chocolate, whisking gently to emulsify. Pour into a clean bowl, cover the surface with clingfilm and refrigerate until required.

For the jelly: Process the raspberries through a juicer, then pass the juice through a fine sieve and measure out 500ml into a bowl.

Make a stock syrup by putting the sugar and 500ml cold water in a saucepan and bring to a simmer, stirring until the sugar has dissolved. Remove from the heat and measure out 350ml.

FOR THIS RECIPE YOU WILL NEED 500ML OF RASPBERRY JUICE. THE SIZE AND RIPENESS OF THE RASPBERRIES WILL DETERMINE HOW MUCH JUICE YOU WILL GET. TO BE SAFE, START WITH 700G RASPBERRIES TO GUARANTEE ENOUGH YIELD.

THE MERINGUE WILL KEEP FOR TWO TO THREE DAYS IN AN AIRTIGHT CONTAINER, BUT IF YOU ADD A LAYER OF SILICA GEL SACHETS TO THE BASE OF THE CONTAINER, IT WILL KEEP FOR UP TO SEVEN DAYS.

Meanwhile, soak the gelatine leaves in ice-cold water for 6 minutes.

Whisk the stock syrup into the 500ml raspberry juice, then mix in the rosewater, adding more to taste if desired. Measure out 100ml, put in a small saucepan and heat gently. Add the drained, squeezed-out gelatine leaves and stir until the gelatine has fully dissolved.

Pass this mixture through a fine sieve back into the remaining raspberry juice mixture and stir thoroughly. Place in the fridge to set for a minimum of 8 hours, preferably overnight.

Whisk the hard-set jelly until it becomes lighter in colour and attains a fluffy texture. Refrigerate the jelly until required.

For the meringue: Preheat the oven to 120°C/gas mark ½. Line two baking trays with silicone paper.

Mix 90g of the sugar thoroughly with the cornflour in a small bowl and set aside.

In the bowl of a stand mixer fitted with the whisk attachment, whisk the egg whites on a high speed until doubled in volume, then reduce the speed to medium and carefully rain in the remaining 175g sugar. Increase the speed to high and whisk for 2–3 minutes. Reduce the speed to medium again and add the vinegar and vanilla extract, then mix for 30 seconds.

Carefully rain in the sugar and cornflour mixture and whisk on a high speed for 1 minute until thick and glossy.

Divide the meringue between the two prepared trays and, using an angled palette knife, spread to a thickness of about 5mm. Generously sprinkle with the dried raspberry pieces.

Bake for 35 minutes, then turn the trays around, reduce the temperature to 110°C/gas mark ¼ and bake for a further 45 minutes, or until the meringue is dry and crispy. The meringue should remain white, so if it starts to colour too much without being fully cooked, reduce the oven temperature by a further 10°C. Remove from the oven and leave to cool completely.

To assemble: This indulgent treat of a dessert can be assembled one of two ways – either in one large trifle dish or in individual coupe glasses. But be sure to serve in a glass container so that all the layers can be seen!

Start by placing the sponge, cut to the required size, into the base of the serving dish, or dishes, and generously soak with the amaretto syrup.

Mix the fresh raspberries with the raspberry purée and spoon a layer on top of the soaked sponge.

Pipe or spoon a layer of the white chocolate custard over the top, then spoon the whisked jelly over, being careful not to leave any custard exposed. You can assemble the dish up to this stage in advance of serving and refrigerate until ready to serve.

Finish by spiking the top of the jelly with shards of the meringue and serve immediately.

WHITE CHOCOLATE + RASPBERRY TRIFLE

TARTE TATIN + CINNAMON CREME FRAICHE

Another classic that's never going to go away, which is great news, as I like it. Not a little, but a lot. It's not going to make you dance on the table, but it's rich and sweet and warm, and will give you a warm and happy feeling.

SERVES 4

FOR THE BUTTERSCOTCH SAUCE
250G LIGHT SOFT BROWN SUGAR
65G SALTED BUTTER, SOFTENED
1 VANILLA POD, SPLIT LENGTHWAYS, AND
    SEEDS SCRAPED OUT

FOR THE TARTE TATIN
250G PUFF PASTRY, DEFROSTED IF FROZEN
PLAIN FLOUR, FOR DUSTING
4 MEDIUM BRITISH EATING APPLES, PEELED,
    HALVED AND CORED
2 VANILLA PODS, SPLIT LENGTHWAYS
CASTER SUGAR, FOR SPRINKLING

TO SERVE
ICING SUGAR, FOR DUSTING
1 TEASPOON GROUND CINNAMON
ABOUT 200ML CREME FRAICHE

Preheat the oven to 180°C/gas mark 4.

For the butterscotch sauce: Heat the sugar in a heavy-based pan over a medium heat until it starts to melt, then stir gently with a heatproof spatula to evenly caramelise the sugar.

Once you have a golden brown caramel, carefully whisk in 50ml cold water over a low heat until the caramel has fully dissolved.

Pass through a sieve into a bowl and leave to cool for 2–3 minutes.

Slowly whisk in the butter and vanilla seeds, then set aside.

For the tarte tatin: Roll the pastry out on a lightly floured work surface to a 35cm disc about the thickness of a pound coin.

Warm the butterscotch sauce in a 30cm ovenproof frying pan, then arrange the apples, cut side facing upwards, and vanilla pods around the pan.

Place the puff pastry disc on top and tuck in the edge of the pastry all round. Sprinkle the pastry with caster sugar.

Bake for 25–30 minutes until golden brown and crisp.

Remove the pan from the oven and leave to rest for 5 minutes.

To serve: Carefully flip the tarte tatin so the pastry is on the bottom, and lightly dust with icing sugar. Whisk the cinnamon into the crème fraîche and serve with the tarte tatin.

TIRAMISU PURNELL'S WAY

Yet another classic pud, this time Italian. As a young commis chef I never really liked it. I think the coffee and the strong alcohol taste were too much for my palate. Although I still feel young and run around like a commis, my taste buds have changed. This has a real grown-up feel, so grow up and try it!

FOR THE COFFEE BAVAROIS
125G MASCARPONE CHEESE
125ML DOUBLE CREAM, PLUS 285ML
3 GELATINE LEAVES
3 MEDIUM EGG YOLKS
45G CASTER SUGAR
12G INSTANT COFFEE GRANULATES

FOR THE CHOCOLATE SORBET
30G GLUCOSE
12G GLYCERINE
150G DARK CHOCOLATE (65 PER CENT
  COCOA SOLIDS), CHOPPED

FOR THE COFFEE SYRUP
125G CASTER SUGAR
5G GROUND COFFEE

FOR THE CHOCOLATE CRUMBLE
210G PLAIN FLOUR
28G COCOA POWDER
55G CASTER SUGAR
110G COLD SALTED BUTTER, DICED

TO SERVE
COCOA POWDER, FOR COATING THE RIMS
STOCK SYRUP (SEE PAGE 143), FOR RUBBING
  THE RIMS OF 6–8 MARTINI GLASSES

For the bavarois: Whip together the mascarpone and 125ml cream in a mixing bowl until soft peaks form, then cover with clingfilm and refrigerate until required.

Soak the gelatine leaves in 1.2 litres cold water for 6 minutes.

In the bowl of a stand mixer fitted with the whisk attachment, whisk the egg yolks and sugar until thick, pale and fluffy.

Pour the remaining 285ml cream into a pan, add the coffee granules and bring to the boil. Remove from the heat, add the drained, squeezed-out gelatine, and stir until dissolved. Pass the mixture through a fine sieve onto the egg yolk mixture and whisk together.

Put the bowl in iced water to cool, but don't allow the mixture to set. When cold, mix into the mascarpone mixture, then transfer to a clean, dry bowl, cover with clingfilm and refrigerate until required.

For the sorbet: Bring 250ml cold water, the glucose and glycerine to the boil in a saucepan. Add the chocolate and whizz with a stick blender.

Put the pan in iced water to cool, then churn in an ice-cream maker according to the manufacturer's instructions until frozen. Store in a lidded freezer-proof container in the freezer for up to 6 months.

For the syrup: Pour 285ml cold water into a pan, mix in the sugar and coffee and heat until the temperature reaches 112°C (use a sugar thermometer). Test the consistency by dipping in a cold spoon and checking whether, on cooling, it is jam like. If not, boil for a further few moments. Remove from the heat and leave to cool.

For the crumble: Preheat the oven to 180°C/gas mark 4.

Mix together the flour, cocoa powder and sugar in a large mixing bowl. Add the butter and rub in with your fingertips until the mixture has a crumb consistency.

Line a baking tray with silicone paper and spread the crumble mixture out on the tray. Bake for 10–15 minutes, turning every couple of minutes, until crumbly. Remove from the oven and leave to cool.

To serve: Spread cocoa powder out onto a saucer.

Rub the rims of 6–8 Martini glasses with the stock syrup then roll the rim of each in the cocoa powder to coat.

Fill the glasses with the coffee bavarois, then spoon the chocolate sorbet on top. Drizzle with the coffee syrup and sprinkle with the chocolate crumble.

SERVES 6–8

to have & to hold, but don't get too kneady

The most important ingredient in bread is love. Bread is probably the most commonly eaten food around the world. It can be the start of the meal or the main part, plus it's a feature of many special occasions. Good bread is a gift. The smell is unbelievable and it's not as difficult as it looks to make. Flat, soda, naan – it's all worth a crack at it. So make it, get your friends around the table and, as they say, break some bread!

BRUMMIE CAKES

Is it a scone, a cake or both? Whatever you call it, it's mustard! It has bacon, cheese, onion and spice, plus Worcestershire sauce is a must (that's where my mom is from). It's a side, it's a snack, it's a main event or just something a little different to eat with your cheese.
I don't know why it is called Brummie cake, it just is!

1 TABLESPOON SUNFLOWER OIL
1 PEELED SHALLOT, DICED
125G SMOKED BACON, CUT INTO LARDONS
300G SELF-RAISING FLOUR, PLUS EXTRA
    FOR DUSTING
1 TEASPOON SALT
25G SALTED BUTTER, DICED
50G MONTGOMERY'S MATURE CHEDDAR
    CHEESE, GRATED
150ML FULL-FAT MILK
1 TABLESPOON TOMATO KETCHUP
5 SPLASHES OF WORCESTERSHIRE SAUCE

Preheat the oven to 170°C/gas mark 3½. Line a baking tray with silicone paper.

Heat the oil in a frying pan, add the shallots and cook over a medium heat for 1 minute without colouring. Add the bacon and cook for 3 minutes until the bacon starts to colour nicely.

Sift together the flour and salt into a mixing bowl. Add the butter and rub in with your fingertips until the mixture has a crumb consistency.

Stir in the bacon and shallots with 20g of the cheese.

In a separate bowl, mix together the milk, ketchup and Worcestershire sauce. Add to the flour mixture and combine with your hands to make a soft dough.

Roll the dough out on a lightly floured work surface into a rough rectangle shape about 1cm in thickness. Using a 6.5cm round cutter, cut the dough into rounds reminiscent of scones and lay on the prepared baking tray, spacing them 5cm apart.

Sprinkle the 'cakes' with the remaining cheese and bake for 20–25 minutes until golden and crisp.

Remove the tray from oven and leave the cakes to cool on the tray for 5 minutes, then carefully transfer to a wire rack to cool completely.

SERVES 6–8

BRUMMIE CAKES

FLATBREAD

Great with salad, Greek food or even a curry, and so easy to buy from the shops – NO! Make your own. It gives you an emotional connection with the world, it's humble, cheap and nothing is better than tucking into fresh, warm bread (well, almost nothing!). Use these as wraps for a BBQ or kids' lunch boxes.

MAKES 6

240G STRONG WHITE BREAD FLOUR, PLUS EXTRA FOR DUSTING
½ TEASPOON SALT
½ TEASPOON CUMIN SEEDS, TOASTED AND GROUND
½ TEASPOON SWEET PAPRIKA
3 TABLESPOONS OLIVE OIL
100ML WARM WATER

Mix together the flour, salt, cumin and paprika in a mixing bowl.

Add the oil to the warm water, then slowly pour into the flour mixture, mixing as you go either with your hands or in a mixer, until it comes together into a heavy dough. Cover the bowl with clingfilm and leave to rest for 20 minutes.

Heat a griddle pan over a medium-high heat.

Divide the dough into six equal balls. Roll out each ball on a lightly floured work surface into a disc 5mm thick.

Cook on the hot griddle pan for 2–3 minutes each side until browned and serve immediately.

BURGER BUNS

It's so cool when you make your own patties but it's even cooler if you make your own baps. Standing there all proud over your BBQ or in your kitchen, flipping your burgers and then sliding them into warm buttery baps. Wow! Who's a clever clogs!

235ML FULL-FAT MILK
55G BUTTER
560G STRONG WHITE BREAD FLOUR, PLUS EXTRA FOR DUSTING
20G FRESH YEAST, CRUMBLED
25G CASTER SUGAR
10G SALT
60G SESAME SEEDS
1 MEDIUM EGG, BEATEN

Combine the milk butter in a saucepan with 120ml cold water and heat until the temperature reaches 50°C (use a sugar thermometer).

Mix two-thirds of the flour (about 375g) with the yeast, sugar, salt and 50g of the sesame seeds in a mixing bowl.

Add the milk mixture to the flour mixture and mix together, then add the remaining flour, a large spoonful at a time, mixing well after each addition, until it is all incorporated.

Knead the dough on a lightly floured board for 5 minutes until smooth and elastic, or use a stand mixer fitted with a dough hook.

Cover the bowl with a clean, damp tea towel and leave the dough to rise for 40 minutes–1 hour, or until doubled in size.

Meanwhile, preheat the oven to 200°C/gas mark 6.

Knock the air out of the dough and divide it into 8 equal pieces.

Shape each piece into a bun shape and place, spaced apart, on a baking tray. Brush with the beaten egg and sprinkle with the remaining sesame seeds.

Bake for 10 minutes, then reduce the temperature to 160°C/gas mark 3 and bake for a further 10 minutes.

Remove from the oven and leave to cool on a wire rack. Serve with a really good burger!

MAKES 8

GRANARY BREAD

Making bread gives you a warm feeling as it rises on the sideboard then goes in the oven to bake. Then there's the smell, the look, peoples' faces when you tell them you've made it. But when you cut into it the next day, toast it and roll butter over the granary brown slice it'll make your mouth water and your eyes will slowly follow, and the smell . . . Amazing!

MAKES 2 900g
LOAVES

400ML WARM WATER
50G FRESH YEAST, CRUMBLED
40G BLACK TREACLE
100ML RAPESEED OR WALNUT OIL
900G GRANARY FLOUR, PLUS EXTRA FOR
    DUSTING
30G TABLE SALT
100G SUNFLOWER SEEDS

Mix together the warm water, yeast, treacle and oil in a bowl until the yeast has dissolved, then leave for 10 minutes until a light froth has formed.

Combine the flour, salt and sunflower seeds in a very large mixing bowl. Make a well in the centre and pour in the yeast mixture, then gradually work in the flour from the sides of the well to create a dough.

Knead the dough on a lightly floured board for 5 minutes until smooth and elastic, or use a stand mixer fitted with a dough hook.

Cover the bowl with a clean, damp tea towel and leave the dough to prove for 20 minutes.

Meanwhile, preheat the oven to 200°C/gas mark 6.

Knock the air out of the dough, then divide equally between two 900g loaf tins.

Bake for 14 minutes, then reduce the temperature to 180°C/gas mark 4 and bake for a further 8 minutes

Remove the tins from the oven, turn the loaves out onto a wire rack and leave to cool.

MILK LOAF

Soft, white, delicate: a perfect breakfast loaf to mop up the bright yellow yolk of a poached egg. Makes me laugh to think about my dad taking the piss because I would have four poached eggs and a small loaf. 'Greedy,' he would say. 'Growing lad,' I would reply. Well, I am 6ft and 14 stone and still growing, Dad!

150ML FULL-FAT MILK
3 CARDAMOM PODS, CRUSHED
20G FRESH YEAST, CRUMBLED
250G STRONG WHITE BREAD FLOUR,
    PLUS EXTRA FOR DUSTING
½ TEASPOON SALT
1 TEASPOON OLIVE OIL

Put the milk, cardamom pods and yeast in a saucepan and warm through.

Remove the pan from the heat and leave for 10 minutes to allow the yeast to dissolve and the cardamom to infuse.

Combine the flour, salt and oil in a mixing bowl. Make a well in the centre and pour in the yeast mixture, then gradually work in the flour with your hands from the sides of the well to create a dough.

Knead the dough on a lightly floured board for 5 minutes until smooth and elastic, or use a stand mixer fitted with a dough hook.

Cover the bowl with a clean, damp tea towel and leave the dough to rise for 45 minutes, or until doubled in size.

Meanwhile, preheat the oven to 200°C/gas mark 6.

Knock the air out of the dough, then put the dough in a 450g loaf tin.

Bake for 10 minutes, then reduce the temperature to 160°C/gas mark 3 and bake for a further 10–12 minutes until golden – it should sound hollow when the base of the bread is tapped.

Turn the loaf out onto a wire rack and leave to cool.

MAKES 1 LOAF

NAAN BREAD

Curry isn't curry without a naan bread. No cutlery, use the bread, that's what I was told as a young lad, and that's how you get the famous yellow fingers. You can't beat a naan bread ... well you can - a table naan, it's massive! It's a bread coat, a bread table cover or a bread duvet!

MAKES 4–6

150ML WARM WATER

10G FRESH YEAST, CRUMBLED

1 TABLESPOON GHEE (OR VEGETABLE OIL OR BUTTER)

PINCH OF CASTER SUGAR

150G STRONG WHITE BREAD FLOUR, PLUS EXTRA FOR KNEADING

50G GRAM FLOUR

1 TABLESPOON SALT, PLUS EXTRA FOR SPRINKLING

1 TABLESPOON CURRY POWDER

1 TABLESPOON CHOPPED CORIANDER LEAVES

70G SALTED BUTTER

Mix together the warm water, yeast, ghee and sugar in a bowl until the yeast has dissolved, then leave for 10 minutes until a light froth has formed.

Combine the flours, salt and curry powder in a mixing bowl. Make a well in the centre and pour in the yeast mixture, then gradually work in the flour from the sides of the well using your hands to create a dough.

Cover the bowl with clingfilm and leave to rest for 1 hour.

Knead a little more flour into the dough on a board, then knead in the coriander.

Divide the dough into 4–6 balls, then roll out each into a rough oval shape to a thickness of 1cm.

Melt the butter in a large frying pan, add the naan breads, in batches, and baste with the butter, then sprinkle with salt. Cook over a medium-high heat for 2 minutes on each side, turning if colouring too fast. Serve immediately.

BANANA BREAD

When I worked for Claude Bosi, he asked me to make banana bread. He loved it and asked me how I'd made it. So I told him – with baking powder. 'Baking powder?' 'Yes chef,' I said. 'Oh really,' he said looking at me hard. 'That's cheating.' Then he ripped a chunk off and plunged it into his coffee. So I made it for his coffee. Oh well, at least he enjoyed it.

MAKES 2
450G LOAVES

KNOB OF BUTTER, FOR GREASING
175G PLAIN FLOUR
150G CASTER SUGAR
2 TEASPOONS BAKING POWDER
½ TEASPOON BICARBONATE OF SODA
½ TEASPOON TABLE SALT
125G SALTED BUTTER, DICED,
4 OVERRIPE BANANAS
1 TEASPOON VANILLA EXTRACT
2 LARGE EGGS

Preheat the oven to 170°C/gas mark 3½. Grease two 450g loaf tins with butter.

Combine the flour and the sugar with the baking powder, bicarbonate of soda and salt in a mixing bowl.

Heat the butter in a saucepan over a medium heat until it turns a nut brown colour – this is called beurre noisette. Be careful not to colour the butter too much and burn it! Remove the pan from the heat.

Put the bananas in a blender and whizz to a smooth purée, then transfer to a bowl. Mix in the beurre noisette and vanilla extract, then beat in the eggs, one at a time.

Add the wet mixture, a spoonful at a time, to the dry mixture and mix until smooth.

Divide the mixture between the prepared tins and bake for 30 minutes, then reduce the temperature to 120°C/gas mark ½ and bake for a further 15 minutes.

Remove the tins from the oven, turn the loaves out onto a wire rack and leave to cool.

SODA BREAD

My good friend Danny Millar, a proud Irish man, is a true gent. Danny served me some amazing soda bread and this is my take on it. I hope he likes it. Also, my Kez loves soda bread and I really hope she likes it too! xxx

500G WHOLEMEAL FLOUR
500G STRONG WHITE BREAD FLOUR, PLUS EXTRA FOR DUSTING
2 TABLESPOONS BICARBONATE OF SODA
1½ TEASPOONS SALT
1 TEASPOON CRACKED BLACK PEPPER
100G SALTED BUTTER, SOFTENED AND DICED
625ML BUTTERMILK

Preheat the oven to 180°C/gas mark 4.

Combine the flours, bicarbonate of soda, salt and black pepper in a large mixing bowl. Add the butter and rub in with your fingertips.

Mix in the buttermilk, kneading to make a dough.

Form into a loaf shape and leave to rest for 10 minutes.

Place the dough on a baking tray, dust with flour and bake for 50 minutes–1 hour until browned.

Remove the tray from the oven, slide the loaf inti a wire rack and leave to cool.

MAKES 1 LOAF

CARAMEL BREAD

Bread made with love is great, adding treacle can only make it better! It gives a lovely depth of colour as well as a sweet and bitter taste. Plus the smell as it cooks is incredible.

425ML WARM WATER
100G FRESH YEAST, CRUMBLED
50G BLACK TREACLE
50G GOLDEN SYRUP
420G STRONG WHITE BREAD FLOUR, PLUS EXTRA FOR DUSTING
410G WHOLEMEAL FLOUR
20G SALT

Mix together the warm water, yeast, black treacle and golden syrup in a bowl until the yeast has dissolved, then leave for 10 minutes until a light froth has formed.

Combine the flours and salt in a large mixing bowl. Make a well in the centre and pour in the yeast mixture, then gradually work in the flour from the sides of the well to create a dough.

Knead the dough on a lightly floured board for 5 minutes until smooth and elastic, or use a stand mixer fitted with a dough hook.

Cover the bowl with a clean, damp tea towel and leave the dough to rise for 30 minutes, or until doubled in size.

Meanwhile, preheat the oven to 200°C/gas mark 6.

Knock the air out of the dough, then divide it in half and form each into a loaf shape. Place on a large baking tray.

Bake for 10 minutes, then reduce the temperature to 160°C/gas mark 3 and bake for a further 14 minutes.

Remove the tray from the oven, slide the loaves onto a wire rack and leave to cool.

MAKES 2 LOAVES

bits & stuff
& cheeky tricks

This cheeky chapter is just bits and stuff and tricks that didn't really fit anywhere else, but I feel they're just as important as the rest. It includes a cocktail or two, some roasting and pickling, and the odd purée, plus some solid stuff too. All of them – the cocktails, the veggies, the sauces – are there for you to try and wow your friends and guests. Some shaken, some stirred. It could even be the most useful chapter of all!

ROASTED SPICED CAULIFLOWER

My memories of cauliflower at home are of my mom boiling it at 8am in the morning on a Sunday and us not eating it until 4 o'clock in the afternoon. What was amazing – I don't know how she did it – was that it stayed in a whole piece but as soon as I touched it with my fork it exploded into water and tasted of nothingness. This dish celebrates the humble cauliflower and turns a side vegetable into a full-time hero!

25G BUTTER
1 TABLESPOON MILD CURRY POWDER
1 TEASPOON GROUND CUMIN
1 TEASPOON GROUND GINGER
½ CINNAMON STICK
3 CLOVES
1 TEASPOON CORIANDER SEEDS
1 TEASPOON FENUGREEK SEEDS
1 TEASPOON DRIED CHILLI FLAKES
1 LARGE CAULIFLOWER, CUT INTO
   SMALL FLORETS
1 LITRE HOT VEGETABLE STOCK, OR ENOUGH
   TO COVER THE CAULIFLOWER

Melt the butter in a saucepan, add all the spices and cook gently for 1 minute.

Add the cauliflower florets and enough vegetable stock to cover and simmer for 20 minutes, or until tender.

Remove the pan from the heat and leave the cauliflower to cool in the stock.

SERVES 6

SPICED MANGO PUREE

Is it a bird? Is it a plane? No, it's mango purée! Is it a sauce or a condiment? That, my friend, is up to you.

4 SMALL RIPE MANGOES
250G GRANULATED SUGAR
250G WHITE WINE VINEGAR
2 TEASPOONS AJWAIN SEEDS
2 TEASPOONS WHITE MUSTARD SEEDS
2 TEASPOONS FENUGREEK SEEDS
2 TEASPOONS BLACK ONION SEEDS
2 TEASPOONS DRIED CHILLI FLAKES
1 BAY LEAF
2 TEASPOONS SALT
1 TEASPOON GROUND GINGER

Peel the mangoes, remove the stones and cut the flesh into small pieces.

Put the sugar, vinegar, ajwain, mustard, fenugreek and black onion seeds and chilli flakes in a saucepan and bring to the boil.

Add the mangoes and bay leaf and simmer for about 20 minutes until the mango is tender.

Strain the mango mixture through a sieve and remove the bay leaf.

Put the mango mixture in a blender with the salt and ginger and whizz until smooth.

Pass the mango purée through a fine sieve.

MAKES 10–15 SERVINGS

ROASTED SPICED CAULIFLOWER
WITH SPICED MANGO PUREE

PICKLED CAULIFLOWER

You can boil it, roast it or fry it. Pickling is also another great way to celebrate the humble cauliflower. Serve hot or cold.

SERVES 6

1 CAULIFLOWER
5 TEASPOONS CURRY POWDER
3 TABLESPOONS GRANULATED SUGAR
1 TEASPOON CUMIN SEEDS
1 TEASPOON GRATED FRESH GINGER
1 BAY LEAF
2 CLOVES
4 CARDAMOM PODS
½ CINNAMON STICK
550ML CHICKEN STOCK
130ML WHITE WINE VINEGAR

Cut the cauliflower into small florets and put in a 1-litre heat-resistant container.

Combine all the remaining ingredients in a saucepan and bring to the boil, then pour over cauliflower.

Leave to cool and then serve.

MUSHROOM DUXELLES

Duxelles is a finely chopped (minced) mixture of mushrooms, onions or shallots, and herbs sautéed in butter and reduced until all the moisture is removed.
I add red wine to add a depth of flavour to the mushrooms. Cream is used at the end to lift the richness and give a less bitter, more rounded, mouth feel.

SERVES 4

700G FIELD MUSHROOMS
30G SALTED BUTTER
30G SHALLOT, FINELY DICED
3G GARLIC, GRATED
100ML RED WINE
SALT AND GROUND WHITE PEPPER

TO SERVE
DOUBLE CREAM
CHOPPED CHIVES

Peel the mushrooms and roughly chop. Put in a food processor and process until very finely chopped.

Heat a saucepan and add the butter. When foaming, add the shallot and garlic and cook over a medium heat for 1 minute without colouring.

Add the finely chopped mushrooms and cook over a gentle heat until the mushrooms release all their liquid, then continue cooking until all the moisture has evaporated.

Stir in the wine and cook until the wine has reduced fully and the duxelles is starting to dry out in the pan. Season to taste with table salt and white pepper.

Transfer the duxelles into a clean container and leave to cool at room temperature. Cover and store in the fridge until required. The duxelles will keep for up to five days.

When serving, put the desired amount of duxelles in a small saucepan and add enough cream just to cover the base of the pan. Heat until the cream has been absorbed then add the chives to taste. Serve immediately.

GNOCCHI

Gnocchi is a fantastic alternative to potatoes or rice. It's a great dish on its own and can be served with meat or fish. My mate Pete and his beautiful wife Nic loved a good bit of gnocchi on a Thursday night.

900G HOT BAKED POTATO FLESH, PASSED
  THROUGH A DRUM SIEVE OR POTATO RICER
175G PARMESAN CHEESE, FINELY GRATED
200G PLAIN FLOUR, PLUS EXTRA
  FOR DUSTING
1 EGG, BEATEN
1 EGG YOLK, BEATEN
SALT AND FRESHLY GROUND BLACK PEPPER
SPLASH OF VEGETABLE OIL
KNOB OF BUTTER
1 TABLESPOON CHOPPED CHIVES

Mix together the potato (while it is still warm), Parmesan, flour, whole egg, egg yolk and salt and black pepper to season in a large mixing bowl to form a dough.

Roll the dough on a lightly floured work surface into sausage shapes about 4cm in diameter, then wrap each one tightly in clingfilm and seal the ends.

Bring a large saucepan of water to a simmer, add the 'sausages' and cook for 17–20 minutes.

Remove the sausages from the pan and put in iced water until completely cold.

Drain the sausages and remove the clingfilm, then slice into rounds about 5mm thick.

Heat the oil and butter in a frying pan and fry the dough rounds for 2–3 minutes on each side until golden.

Serve basted with the pan juices and sprinkled with the chives.

SERVES 6

GREEN BEANS FRENCH STYLE

300G FINE GREEN BEANS, TOPPED
   AND TAILED
3 TABLESPOONS OLIVE OIL
2 GARLIC CLOVES, CRUSHED
2 MEDIUM SHALLOTS, DICED
1 TABLESPOON SHERRY VINEGAR
2 SPRIGS OF THYME
ROCK SALT AND FRESHLY GROUND
   BLACK PEPPER
1 TABLESPOON CHOPPED TARRAGON

Bring a saucepan of water to the boil, add the beans and blanch for 2 minutes.

Drain the beans and immediately plunge into iced water and leave until cool, then drain.

Warm the oil in a sauté pan (don't overheat), add the garlic and shallots and cook over a gentle heat for 3 minutes.

Strain the oil through a sieve, returning the garlic and shallots to the pan, and reserve the oil.

Add the vinegar and thyme to the garlic and shallots, then the beans and warm through.

Season with salt and black pepper, then cover with the reserved oil. Sprinkle over the tarragon and serve.

SERVES 4

BUTTER ROASTED CABBAGE

1 MEDIUM CABBAGE (HISPI, SPRING OR
   SWEETHEART)
250G BUTTER
1 TABLESPOON PINK PEPPERCORNS, CRUSHED
1 LIME, CUT IN HALF, FOR SQUEEZING

Preheat the oven to 160°C/gas mark 3.

Cut the cabbage in half lengthways.

Melt the butter in a large flameproof casserole dish, add the cabbage, cut-side down, and cook until lightly browned.

Using a large spoon, baste the cabbage with the foaming butter, then add the peppercorns.

Cover the dish with the lid and place in the oven for 15 minutes.

Remove from the oven and baste again, then re-cover and return to the oven to roast for a further 15 minutes. Repeat the process of basting and roasting for about 30 minutes until the cabbage is tender.

When the cabbage is cooked, squeeze over the lime and serve in the middle of the table.

SERVES 4

BRAISED ONIONS

SERVES 2

SPLASH OF VEGETABLE OIL
2 ONIONS, SKIN ON, CUT IN HALF
4 GARLIC CLOVES
100G BUTTER
2 SPRIGS OF THYME
2 SPRIGS OF ROSEMARY
1 BAY LEAF
400ML HOT VEGETABLE STOCK
1 TABLESPOON CHOPPED CHIVES
1 TABLESPOON CHOPPED PARSLEY
1 TABLESPOON CHOPPED CHERVIL
1 TABLESPOON CHOPPED SAGE

Preheat the oven to 180°C/gas mark 4.

Heat the oil in a flameproof, ovenproof dish, add the onions, cut-side down, and cook until browned.

Add the garlic, butter, thyme, rosemary and bay leaf and cook until the butter is foaming, then pour over the vegetable stock.

Cover the dish with foil and place in the oven for 20–25 minutes until the onions 'give' to the tip of a knife.

Remove the dish from the oven and set aside for 5 minutes.

Meanwhile, mix the herbs together.

Turn the onions out onto a serving board, glaze with the cooking liquid and sprinkle with the mixed herbs. Serve each half onion with a garlic clove.

CARROTS COOKED IN BLACK TREACLE

SERVES 4

125G BLACK TREACLE
125G BUTTER
4 CARDAMOM PODS, CRACKED
12–16 BABY CARROTS, WASHED AND UNPEELED

Melt the black treacle and butter in a deep pan.

Add the cardamom pods, carrots and 500ml cold water, cover the pan with a lid and simmer for 10 minutes, or until the carrots are tender.

Remove the carrots and set aside, then cook the cooking liquid until reduced by half.

Cover the carrots with the reduction and serve.

POMMES BOULANGÈRES

SERVES 6–8

1.5KG MEDIUM–LARGE POTATOES (DESIREE, MARIS PIPER OR KING EDWARD ARE BEST)
2 LARGE ONIONS
1 TABLESPOON VEGETABLE OIL
75G SALTED BUTTER
1 GARLIC CLOVE, FINELY CHOPPED
10 SPRIGS OF THYME
3 TABLESPOONS SHERRY VINEGAR OR WHITE WINE VINEGAR
SALT AND FRESHLY GROUND BLACK PEPPER
750ML LAMB STOCK (SEE PAGE 184) (OR BROWN CHICKEN STOCK, SEE PAGE 184)

Preheat the oven to 180°C/gas mark 4.

Peel the potatoes, then thinly slice using a mandoline and soak in a large bowl of cold water for 1 hour.

Drain the potato slices well, rinse, then pat dry between two clean tea towels.

Cut the onions in half and thinly slice using the mandoline.

Heat the oil in a large frying pan, add half the butter and heat until the butter is foaming, then add the onions and garlic with four sprigs of thyme and sauté for about 10 minutes, stirring once or twice.

Add the vinegar and cook until all the liquid has evaporated, stirring occasionally so that the onions don't catch.

Arrange a quarter of the potato slices in a large ovenproof dish approximately 30 x 15cm. Season with salt and black pepper, then sprinkle over leaves from three thyme sprigs and scatter over one-third of the onions. Repeat the potato and onion layers three more times, seasoning in between. Then finish with just a potato layer and the thyme leaves from the remaining three sprigs.

Melt the remaining butter in a small saucepan.

Bring the stock to the boil in a separate saucepan, then ladle it over the potatoes and onions, ensuring that it seeps down the sides. Brush the top with the melted butter, then bake for 45 minutes–1 hour until golden on top.

FRITES

2KG CHIPPING POTATOES, PEELED AND SLICED ON A MANDOLINE USING THE THICK SHREDDER
SALT
VEGETABLE OIL, FOR DEEP-FRYING

Blanch the potato slices in a saucepan of salted boiling water for 1 minute, then drain and lay out over a large tray lined with a clean, new J-cloth and leave to air-dry for 5 minutes. Once dry, either cook immediately or refrigerate for later.

Deep-fry the potato slices, in batches, until golden brown and crispy. Remove from the oil, drain on kitchen paper and season with salt. Serve immediately – never re-fry.

RED WINE SAUCE

SERVES 4

SPLASH OF VEGETABLE OIL
2 SHALLOTS, ROUGHLY DICED
2 GARLIC CLOVES, ROUGHLY CHOPPED
2 TOMATOES, QUARTERED
2 SPRIGS OF THYME
400ML RED WINE
1 LITRE HOT BEEF STOCK

Heat the oil in a large saucepan, add the shallots and garlic and cook over a medium heat until golden brown.

Add the tomatoes and thyme and cook for a further 5 minutes.

Stir in the wine and cook until reduced to a glaze consistency.

Add the beef stock and cook until reduced to 300ml.

Remove the pan from the heat and pass the sauce through a fine sieve.

BORDELAISE SAUCE

SERVES 4

SPLASH OF VEGETABLE OIL
1 BANANA SHALLOT, FINELY DICED
800ML RED WINE SAUCE (SEE ABOVE)
¼ BUNCH OF PARSLEY, LEAVES PICKED AND
   FINELY CHOPPED
50G BONE MARROW (ASK YOUR BUTCHER),
   CUT INTO CUBES

Heat the oil in a saucepan, add the shallot and sweat over a gentle heat until softened but not coloured.

Stir in the red wine sauce and parsley.

Using a blowtorch, colour the bone marrow evenly all over, being careful that the fat doesn't spit everywhere.

Add the marrow to the sauce and bring to the boil, then remove from the heat.

CURRY SAUCE

SERVES 6–8

SPLASH OF VEGETABLE OIL
2 MEDIUM ONIONS, CHOPPED
4 GARLIC CLOVES, CHOPPED
1 TABLESPOON MILD CURRY POWDER
KNOB OF BUTTER
2 BAY LEAVES
180G POTATOES (ANY SEASONAL TYPE),
   PEELED AND CHOPPED
200ML WHITE WINE
500ML HOT CHICKEN STOCK OR
   BOILING WATER
300ML DOUBLE CREAM

Heat the oil in a saucepan, add the onions and sweat over a gentle heat until softened but not coloured.

Add the garlic, curry powder, butter and bay leaves and sweat for 3 minutes.

Stir in the potatoes and wine and cook until the wine has reduced by two-thirds.

Stir in the chicken stock and the water and simmer for about a further 15 minutes until the potatoes are cooked.

Add the cream and cook for another 5 minutes.

Remove the bay leaves, pour the mixture into a blender and whizz until smooth, then pass through a fine sieve.

LAMB STOCK

MAKES 3 LITRES

2 LEEKS, WASHED AND ROUGHLY CHOPPED
4 CELERY STICKS, ROUGHLY CHOPPED
2 ONIONS, ROUGHLY CHOPPED
6 CARROTS, PEELED AND ROUGHLY CHOPPED
6 LARGE FIELD MUSHROOMS, CLEANED AND
    ROUGHLY CHOPPED
6 TOMATOES, ROUGHLY CHOPPED
1 GARLIC BULB, ROUGHLY CHOPPED
1KG LAMB BONES
½ BUNCH OF THYME
½ BUNCH OF ROSEMARY
200ML BRANDY
400ML WHITE WINE

Preheat the oven to 180°C/gas mark 4.

Spread the vegetables out in a large roasting tin, then place the lamb bones, evenly distributed, on top.

Roast for 40–50 minutes until golden brown.

Remove the tin from the oven and transfer the roasted bones and vegetables to a stock pot, along with the herbs. Discard any remaining fat in the tin.

Set the roasting tin on the hob over a high heat and deglaze with the brandy, scraping up all the sediment with a wooden spoon, and cook to evaporate the alcohol.

Add the wine and cook to evaporate the alcohol while scraping up any leftover sediment from the tin.

Add the contents of the tin to the stock pot, cover with 3 litres cold water and bring to the boil, skimming off any impurities that rise to the surface.

Reduce the heat and simmer for 2–4 hours, skimming frequently.

Remove the pan from the heat and pass the stock through a fine sieve into a bowl, discarding all the bones, vegetables and herbs, then pass the stock through a muslin cloth.

Cook the stock until reduced by half, then remove the pan from the heat, leave to cool, cover and refrigerate.

BROWN CHICKEN STOCK

MAKES 3 LITRES

1KG CHICKEN BONES, CHOPPED (ASK YOUR
    BUTCHER)
500G CHICKEN WINGS
1 GARLIC BULB, CUT IN HALF HORIZONTALLY
2 ONIONS, PEELED AND CUT IN HALF
2 CARROTS, PEELED AND ROUGHLY CHOPPED
3 CELERY STICKS, ROUGHLY CHOPPED
1 LEEK, CUT IN HALF LENGTHWAYS, WASHED
    AND ROUGHLY CHOPPED
2 FIELD MUSHROOMS, CLEANED AND
    ROUGHLY CHOPPED
½ BUNCH OF THYME
1 BAY LEAF
375ML WHITE WINE

Preheat the oven to 200°C/gas mark 6.

Put the chicken bones and wings and all the vegetables in a large roasting tin (or divide between two if necessary).

Roast for 40–50 minutes until golden brown, turning occasionally to achieve an even colour.

Remove the tin from the oven and transfer the roasted bones and wings and vegetables to a stock pot, along with the thyme and bay leaf.

Set the roasting tin on the hob over a high heat and deglaze with the wine, scraping up all the sediment with a wooden spoon.

Add the contents of the tin to the stock pot, cover with 3 litres cold water and bring to the boil, skimming off any impurities that rise to the surface.

Reduce the heat and simmer for 4 hours, skimming frequently.

Remove the pan from the heat, pass the stock through a fine sieve into a bowl, discarding all the bones, vegetables and herbs. Leave to cool, then cover with clingfilm and refrigerate. The fat will then solidify and be easy to remove.

FISH STOCK

1KG FISH BONES INCLUDING HEADS,
    CHOPPED (ASK YOUR FISHMONGER)
1 GARLIC BULB, CUT IN HALF HORIZONTALLY
1 ONION, CUT IN HALF
2 CARROTS, PEELED AND ROUGHLY
    CHOPPED
3 CELERY STICKS, ROUGHLY CHOPPED
1 LEEK, CUT IN HALF LENGTHWAYS, WASHED
    AND ROUGHLY CHOPPED
1 FENNEL BULB, ROUGHLY CHOPPED
375ML WHITE WINE
½ BUNCH OF PARSLEY
1 BAY LEAF

Wash the fish bones and heads of any impurities and blood, then put in a large stock pot with all the vegetables and wine.

Cover with 3 litres cold water (or enough to cover the bones), add the parsley and bay leaf and bring to the boil, skimming off any impurities that rise to the surface.

Reduce the heat and simmer for 30 minutes.

Remove the pan from the heat, pass the stock through a fine sieve in a bowl, discarding all the bones, vegetables and herbs. Leave to cool, then cover with clingfilm and refrigerate.

MAKES **3 LITRES**

BROWN VEAL STOCK

3 ONIONS, CUT IN HALF
2 GARLIC BULBS, CUT IN HALF
    HORIZONTALLY
1KG VEAL BONES, CHOPPED (ASK YOUR
    BUTCHER)
2 CARROTS, PEELED AND ROUGHLY
    CHOPPED
3 CELERY STICKS, ROUGHLY CHOPPED
1 LEEK, CUT IN HALF LENGTHWAYS, WASHED
    AND ROUGHLY CHOPPED
2 FIELD MUSHROOMS, CLEANED AND
    ROUGHLY CHOPPED
½ BUNCH OF THYME
1 BAY LEAF
375ML RED WINE

Preheat the oven to 200°C/gas mark 6.

Heat a frying pan over a medium heat, add 1 onion and 1 garlic bulb, cut-side down, and cook until the flesh is blackened.

Put the bones and remaining vegetables in a large roasting tin (or divide between two smaller tins if necessary).

Roast for 40–50 minutes until golden brown, turning occasionally to achieve an even colour.

Remove the tin from the oven and transfer the roasted bones and vegetables to a stock pot, along with the blackened onion and garlic, thyme and bay leaf.

Set the roasting tin on the hob over a high heat and deglaze with the wine, scraping up all the sediment with a wooden spoon.

Add the contents of the tin to the stock pot, cover with 3 litres cold water and bring to the boil, skimming off any impurities that rise to the surface.

Reduce the heat and simmer for 4 hours, skimming frequently.

Remove the pan from the heat, pass the stock through a fine sieve into a bowl, discarding all the bones, vegetables and herbs. Leave to cool, then cover with clingfilm and refrigerate. The fat will then solidify and be easy to remove.

MAKES **3 LITRES**

SCORCHED LEMON
+VANILLA MARGARITA
RHYTHM+BLOOMS COCKTAIL
CELERY POP!

ALEXANDER
HONEY+PEAR CONFIGURATION
OLD FASHIONED PLUM DAQUIRI
'THYME' FOR PIMM'S!

SCORCHED LEMON + VANILLA MARGARITA

I am a tall, burly, hairy man, so you wouldn't think cocktails would be my bag, but you would be wrong! I am a good-time guy, so cocktails all around! Scorched Lemon and Vanilla Margarita is my favourite. The sweet yet salty flavour is great, but for me it's the sour of the lemon with the caramelised flavour that's the winner!

SERVES 4

1 TABLESPOON SEA SALT
4 TABLESPOONS CASTER SUGAR
½ LARGE LEMON, PLUS 4 SLICES
   TO GARNISH
160ML VANILLA TEQUILA (SEE BELOW)
80ML TRIPLE SEC (SUCH AS COINTREAU)
100ML FRESHLY SQUEEZED LEMON JUICE
60ML VANILLA SYRUP (SEE BELOW)
ICE CUBES

FOR THE VANILLA TEQUILA
1 X 50CL BOTTLE OF TEQUILA
2 VANILLA PODS, SPLIT LENGTHWAYS

FOR THE VANILLA SYRUP
300G CASTER SUGAR
1 VANILLA POD, SPLIT LENGTHWAYS

For the vanilla tequila, add the vanilla pods to the bottle of tequila, replace the cap and shake well.

Leave to infuse for a minimum of 24 hours – the longer the better.

For the vanilla syrup, warm the sugar and vanilla pod in 300ml water in a saucepan, stirring until the sugar has dissolved.

Strain and leave to cool. Store in an airtight bottle in the fridge for up to 3 months.

Chill four cocktail glasses.

Mix together the salt and sugar on a saucer.

Cut the lemon half into quarters and again into eighths. Use two of the wedges to rub the rims of the cocktail glasses, then roll the rim of each in the salt and sugar mixture to coat. Keep chilled.

Place the remaining lemon wedges and slices on a metal tray and scorch with a blowtorch.

Using a muddler or heavy spoon, pound the scorched lemon wedges in a Boston cocktail shaker, then add all the other ingredients to the shaker with a handful of ice and shake for a couple of minutes.

Strain into the chilled cocktail glasses and serve each with a scorched lemon slice.

RHYTHM +BLOOMS COCKTAIL

SERVES 1

1 LARGE TOMATO
½ CUCUMBER
35ML HENDRICK'S GIN
20ML ST-GERMAIN ELDERFLOWER LIQUEUR
20ML FRESHLY SQUEEZED LEMON JUICE
10ML (BELVOIR) ELDERFLOWER CORDIAL
SLICE OF CUCUMBER, TO GARNISH

The day before you wish to serve, put the tomato and cucumber in a blender and whizz to a purée. Pass through a fine sieve, pour into three compartments of an ice-cube tray. Freeze overnight.

Pour the remaining ingredients into a mixing glass and stir with a spoon for 1 minute.

Unmould the three tomato and cucumber ice cubes into a serving glass, pour over the cocktail and garnish with a slice of cucumber.

CELERY POP!

SERVES 15

100G SEA SALT (FLEUR DE SEL)
40 CELERY STICKS
5 GRANNY SMITH APPLES

Bring the salt and 4 litres cold water to the boil in a large saucepan. Add the celery and blanch 20 seconds, then immediately drain and refresh in iced water.

Drain the celery, process through a juicer, then pass through a muslin cloth or fine sieve and set aside.

Process the apples in the juicer.

Mix together 1 litre celery juice and 500ml apple juice (the proportions can be varied according to taste, such as half apple to celery). Serve chilled in glasses or little bottles.

HONEY + PEAR CONFIGURATION

SERVES 1

25ML ABSOLUT PEAR-FLAVOURED VODKA
25ML EDMOND BRIOTTET CRÈME DE FIGUE
30ML FRESHLY SQUEEZED LEMON JUICE
15ML SUGAR SYRUP
1½ TEASPOONS RUNNY HONEY
ICE CUBES
SPRIG OF THYME
TWIST OF LEMON

Add all the ingredients to a Boston cocktail shaker with a handful of ice and shake vigorously until the liquid inside is cold.

Cover the shaker with a hawthorne strainer, pour the contents through a fine sieve into a coupette glass. Garnish with thyme and lemon.

_____

ALEXANDER

SERVES 1

40ML BRANDY
ICE CUBES
20ML WHITE CRÈME DE CACAO
20ML DOUBLE CREAM
GRATED NUTMEG, FOR SPRINKLING

Pour the brandy into a Boston cocktail shaker, add a handful of ice, the crème de cacao and cream and shake for 30 seconds.

Using a hawthorne strainer, strain into a Martini glass.

Sprinkle with ground nutmeg and serve.

OLD FASHIONED PLUM DAIQUIRI

SERVES 1

ICE CUBES
20ML APPLETON ESTATE VX RUM
20ML OVD RUM
15ML FRESHLY SQUEEZED LIME JUICE
3 DASHES MAPLE SYRUP
1 DASH PLUM BITTERS
3 THIN SLICES OF PLUM

Fill a mixing glass three-quarters full with ice and add all the remaining ingredients. Stir steadily with a bar spoon for 30 seconds.

Pour into a clean jam jar and serve.

_____

'THYME' FOR PIMM'S!

SERVES 1

ICE CUBES
35ML THYME-INFUSED GIN
30ML PIMM'S
25ML FRESHLY SQUEEZED LEMON JUICE
25ML VANILLA SYRUP (SEE OPPOSITE)
DASH OF STRAWBERRY PUREE
SLICE OF ORANGE
SPRIG OF THYME

Fill a Boston cocktail shaker three-quarters full with ice and add all the remaining ingredients.

Shake for 10–20 seconds, then strain into a sling glass.

Garnish with orange and thyme.

INDEX

a

Alexander 189
almonds: almond ice cream 138
    almond satay 80
apples: pigs' cheeks with apple purée
    103
    roast monkfish tails with buttered
    lettuce, + frozen apple 63
    tarte tatin + cinnamon crème
    fraîche 146
    turbot with squid rolled in crispy
    pork, apple + tarragon purée 76
apricots, sablé Breton with almond
    ice cream + roasted 138
artichokes: sea bass with pistou,
    artichokes + sun-dried tomatoes 74
asparagus, tartare of 25

b

baked Alaska, Christmas easy 121
Balearic prawns with chilli butter 28
bananas: banana bread 166
    banana 'non'-ice cream 115
beef: beef rendang 110
    50/50 burger 106
    rump steak with baked potato
    gratin 104
biscotti, pistachio + hazelnut 128
blackberry parfait 134
bread 156–67
    Ma's bread + butter pudding 135
Brummie cakes 153
burgers, 50/50 106

c

cabbage, butter roasted 177
caramel bread 167
carrots cooked in black treacle 178
cauliflower: pickled cauliflower 174
    roasted spiced cauliflower 171
celery pop! 189
cheese: cheese + potato pie 'gratin' 26
    red mullet with ceps + goats' cheese 78
    roast chicken thighs with Mortadella

sausage, feta + black olives 85
cheesecake, white + dark chocolate 115
cherry clafoutis 137
chicken: brown chicken stock 184
    chicken goujons 42
    chicken supreme 86
    grilled Szechuan-style chicken
    skewers 38
    roast chicken thighs with
    Mortadella sausage, feta + black
    olives 85
    salt + pepper chicken wings 45
chicory, fenugreek-glazed 100
chillies: chilli butter 28
    chilli lemon + rosemary savoury
    popcorn 37
    chilli peanut noodles 46
chocolate: gâteau liégeois, GP style 141
    poached summer fruits in basil
    + cardamom with sabayon + white
    chocolate 126
    tiramisu Purnell's way 149
    white + dark chocolate cheesecake 115
    white chocolate + raspberry trifle
    142–3
Christmas easy-baked Alaska 121
clafoutis, cherry 137
clams, baked hake + 60
cobbler, ox cheek 109
cocktails 188–9
cod: baked cod with a secret green
    crust 57
coffee: gâteau liégeois, GP style 141
    tiramisu Purnell's way 149
confit lemon + vanilla pork belly 93
couscous, pomegranate 86
cranberry meringue 129
crème brûlée 119
curry: curry sauce 182
    Malaysian fish curry 68

d

daiquiri, old fashioned plum 189
dried fruit: muesli, seeds + fruit mix
14
duck: duck rillettes 32
    duck spring rolls 46
    duck with spiced plum jam 90
    Purnell's Peking duck 97
    roast duck breasts with goats' curd
    + elderflower, peas + radishes 96

e

eclairs 124–5
eggs: double cream scrambled eggs
    with smoked salmon, salmon eggs

+ watercress 23
    egg yolk + salmon tartlets 18
    oeufs cocotte 17
    potato omelette with smoked
    salmon 20

f

fennel: green fennel juice 15
    tartare of asparagus + fennel cloud 25
fenugreek-glazed chicory 100
50/50 burger 106
fish: fish stock 185
    Malaysian fish curry 68
    see also cod; hake, etc
flatbread 156
fruit: fast fruit frumble 128
    poached summer fruits in basil
    + cardamom 126
    sweet fruit salad 11–12
    see also dried fruit

g

gâteau liégeois, GP style 141
gnocchi 175
goats' curd, roast duck breasts with 96
gratins: baked potato gratin 104
    cheese + potato pie 26
green beans, French style 177
green juice 15
gremolata 66

h

haddock: smoked haddock with
    crème fraîche mash 69
hake: baked hake + clams in green
    sauce 60
hazelnuts: pistachio + hazelnut
    biscotti 128

i

ice cream, almond 138

j

juices 15

l

lamb: caramelised, slow-cooked lamb 98
    lamb stock 184
    roast rack of lamb with orange 100
lemons: chilli lemon + rosemary
    savoury popcorn 37
    confit lemon + vanilla pork belly 93
    scorched lemon + vanilla margarita 188
limes, scallops with 64

m

Malaysian fish curry 68
mango purée, spiced 171
margarita, scorched lemon + vanilla 188
Ma's bread + butter pudding 135
meringues: cranberry meringue 129
  passion fruit parfait with crispy meringue 122
monkfish: roast monkfish tails with buttered lettuce + frozen apple 63
Mortadella sausage: roast chicken thighs with Mortadella sausage, feta + black olives 85
muesli, seeds + fruit mix 14
mushrooms: mushroom duxelles 174
  mussels in cider with parsley + trumpet mushrooms 73
  red mullet with ceps + goats' cheese 78
mussels in cider with parsley + trumpet mushrooms 73

n

naan bread 164
noodles: chilli peanut noodles 46
  egg noodles with potted shrimps 48
  roast salmon with salsa verde, noodles + gremolata 66

o

oeufs cocotte 17
omelette: potato omelette with smoked salmon 20
orange, roast rack of lamb with 100
ox cheek cobbler 109

p

parfaits: blackberry parfait 134
  passion fruit parfait 122
Paris-Brest 132
passion fruit parfait 122
peanuts: chilli peanut noodles 46
pears, blackberry parfaits with poached 134
peppers: spiced red pepper + tomato soup 22
pickled cauliflower 174
Pimm's, 'thyme' for 189
pineapple: pineapple skewers 118
  salt-baked pineapple 93
piperade, roast scallops with 77
pistachio + hazelnut biscotti 128
pistou, sea bass with 74
pomegranate couscous 86

popcorn, chilli lemon + rosemary savoury 37
pork: confit lemon + vanilla pork belly 93
  50/50 burger 106
  pigs' cheeks with apple purée, crispy pork, hispi cabbage + lettuce 103
  spiced pork belly with grilled pak choi 92
  sweet spicy sticky ribs 52
  turbot with squid rolled in crispy pork, apple + tarragon purée 76
potatoes: baked potato gratin 104
  cheese + potato pie 'gratin' 26
  crème fraîche mash 69
  frites 180
  gnocchi 175
  pommes boulangères 180
  potato omelette with smoked salmon 20
  salt-baked potatoes 49
prawns: Balearic prawns with chilli butter 28
  crispy scallop + prawn balls 41
profiteroles 124–5
Purnell's Peking duck 97

r

rabbit: sweet + sour bunny 89
raspberries: white chocolate + raspberry trifle 142–3
red juice 15
red mullet with ceps + goats' cheese 78
rendang, beef 110
rhubarb: frozen rhubarb + cranberry meringue 129
rhythm + blooms cocktail 188
rillettes, duck 32

s

sabayon 126
sablé Breton 138
salad, sweet fruit 11–12
salmon: double cream scrambled eggs with smoked salmon, salmon eggs + watercress 23
  egg yolk + salmon tartlets 18
  potato omelette with smoked salmon 20
  roast salmon with salsa verde, noodles + gremolata 66
salsa verde 66
sauces 182
scallops: crispy scallop + prawn balls 41
  roast scallops with piperade 77
  scallops with lime, wasabi crumble + watercress 64

scallops with raw vegetables, almond satay + ponzu 80
sea bass with pistou, artichokes + sun-dried tomatoes 74
seeds: muesli, seeds + fruit mix 14
shrimps, egg noodles with potted 48
skewers: pineapple skewers 118
  Szechuan-style chicken skewers 38
smoked haddock with crème fraîche mash 69
soda bread 167
soups: spiced red pepper + tomato soup 22
  tom yum soup 31
spring rolls, duck 46
squid: scorched baby squid Provençal 70
  turbot with squid rolled in crispy pork, apple + tarragon purée 76
stocks 184–5

t

tartare of asparagus + fennel cloud 25
tarts: egg yolk + salmon tartlets 18
  tarte tatin 146
'thyme' for Pimm's! 189
tiramisu Purnell's way 149
tom yum soup 31
tomatoes: spiced red pepper + tomato soup 22
trifle, white chocolate + raspberry 142–3
turbot with squid rolled in crispy pork, apple + tarragon purée 76

v

veal stock, brown 185
vegetables, scallops with raw 80

w

wasabi crumble 64
wine sauce, red 182

ACKNOWLEDGEMENTS

Kyle Cathie. Thank you for giving me another crack at a book. I hope I didn't let you down.

Judith Hannam. The coolest editor in the business! So calm, a pleasure to work with.

Peter Cassidy. A gent who oozes passion for food and photography, amazing job. Thank you.

Rosie Reynolds. What can I say? You nailed it again.
                    Your gentle touch with a Scouse accent – unbeatable.

Helen Bratby. Wow, such great colour and arrangement. Perfectly put together.

Iris Bromet. The props and plates were fab and made the food sing!

Thanks to Agg for the second time around, for translating my awful writing into text.

Thank you to Luke Butcher, my right hand man. And to Sam Luckett, Phil Steggall,
Tom 'The Cheese' Blakemore and David Taylor for all their input.

Martine Carter. A great agent. Not a secret one, a brilliant one!

The item should be returned or renewed by the last date stamped below.

Dylid dychwelyd neu adnewyddu'r eitem erbyn y dyddiad olaf sydd wedi'i stampio isod

PILLGWENLLY

To renew visit / Adnewyddwch ar
www.newport.gov.uk/libraries

The Story
of the
Forest